The

Herb

Bible

The
Herb
Bible

Stefan Buczacki

**The definitive guide
to choosing and
growing herbs**

MITCHELL
BEAZLEY

An Hachette UK Company
www.hachette.co.uk

First published in Great Britain in 2015 by Mitchell Beazley,
a division of Octopus Publishing Group Ltd,
Endeavour House, 189 Shaftesbury Avenue,
London WC2H 8JY
www.octopusbooks.co.uk

This book contains revised and updated material from *Best Herbs*.

Distributed in the US by Hachette Book Group
1290 Avenue of the Americas, 4th and 5th Floors,
New York, NY 10020

Distributed in Canada by Canadian Manda Group
664 Annette St., Toronto, Ontario, Canada M6S 2C8

Stefan Buczacki asserts the moral right to be identified as the author of this work.

ISBN 978-1-84533-926-5

A CIP catalogue record for this book is available from the British Library.
Printed and bound in China.
10 9 8 7 6 5 4 3 2 1

Contents

TEMPERATURE CHART

BARELY HARDY	0° to -5°C	(32° to 23°F)
FAIRLY HARDY	-5° to -10°C	(23° to 14°F)
MODERATELY HARDY	-10° to -15°C	(14° to 5°F)
HARDY	-15° to -20°C	(5° to -4°F)
VERY HARDY	-20°C or below	(-4°F or below)

ALL ABOUT HERBS

What Is a Herb?

It's an interesting word, herb, with different meanings for different people. And as I have described some plants that might be thought to be surprising inclusions in a herb book, while just possibly having omitted one or two that might have been expected, you are entitled to an explanation.

To a botanist, the word herb is shorthand for the term herbaceous plant, which is one that differs from a tree or a shrub in lacking any woody framework and more or less dies down in the autumn to survive the winter as a rootstock. But clearly that definition won't suffice for present purposes as there are several shrubs and some trees in the book. As the name derives from Latin, through French, do those languages help us? Not much. *Herba* in Latin means grass, or more or less any green plant, while to the French, *une herbe* is simply a plant, more specifically a grass, and often modified in such terms as *herbe marine* (seaweed) or *mauvaise herbe* (weed).

The first recorded use of 'herb' in English specifically to mean a plant that has some culinary or medicinal value was in 1290 and subsequently Chaucer used it too but even today, it is employed with varying scope. Thyme is generally recognized as a kitchen herb, but what about parsley; sage is generally perceived as a herb but what about onion? And where do lettuce and celery fit in; or apple and blackcurrant? Where do vegetables and fruit end and herbs begin? I don't know, and so I've devised my own definitions and, as far as culinary use is concerned, I've included only those plants that are used principally to add specific flavours to dishes and meals without being major edible components in their own right. So parsley and some types of onion are in; but lettuce and apple are out.

Not all herbs, however, are culinary; indeed some are poisonous but are used, or have been used in the past, for medicinal purposes. I have included a large number of species that fall into this category. By and large, however, I have left out those plants whose only use has been as a source of dyes, for this is a large, rather complex and specialized subject that is of

Above: *Woven willow beds with chives and contrasting fennel.*
Left: *Rosemary growing in a narrow mixed border.*

interest only to a very small number of gardeners. I have also generally excluded plants that qualify solely for what I may best call household uses such as pan scouring, pest control or even potpourri, for which it seems almost every scented plant under the sun has been used at one time or another. Which brings me to my final

point. This is a gardening book, not a cookbook or a medicinal herbal. I have written from the standpoint of a gardener who wants to grow a range of herbs to use in the kitchen but who also has an interest in those many others with medicinal roles, without being likely to ever want to try them. So while I have indicated the general kitchen uses, I have given no recipes. And even more importantly, I have given no details of the way that herb plants are prepared for medicinal use and must emphasize that this is not something to be undertaken without expert guidance and knowledge.

Above: *A herb garden with flowering chives creates a peaceful retreat in which to stop and sit.*

So, I hope you will grow a large number of herbs in your garden, will find many of them attractive in their own right, will enjoy using some in your cooking and will find much interest in familiarizing yourself with those that have, over the years, performed intriguing and sometimes remarkable medicinal roles.

Site and Soil

Herbs are rather more demanding in respect of their soil and site requirements than many of the plants that you will grow in your garden. Although there are some notable exceptions, it's fair to say that most grow best in light, fairly free-draining, alkaline and not very rich soils; and in full sun.

Above: *Thyme intersperses* Sempervivum *and* Stachys byzantina *in this coastal rock garden.*

Of course, not all gardeners have these conditions but because herb gardens are generally fairly small, it is usually possible to alter the existing soil to bring it closer to the optimum, even if this means creating a small raised bed in which to do it. There is little that can be done if your garden beds are all shady, although even there, it may be feasible to grow some herbs in containers on a sunny patio or path edge, as described on page 24.

Before you can begin to amend your soil, you really need to understand how different soils vary and how many changes can and cannot be made. All soils are made up of differing amounts of clay, silt and humus. (Stones and pebbles don't play a part in this although a

soil with plenty of pebbles in it is no bad thing for herb growing as the pebbles will usefully help to retain heat.) A soil that contains a high proportion of clay will be slow to warm up in spring but then stays warm and will also contain a good supply of nutrients. In dry conditions, however, clay soils will become hard and impenetrable whereas in the wet winter weather, they may become waterlogged; precisely the wrong conditions for herbs. By contrast, a light, sandy soil will warm up quickly, cool down quickly and, being free-draining, lose both water and nutrients rapidly. Humus, which is simply part-decomposed organic matter, will improve both types of soil because it contains natural gel-like substances that bind together soil particles to form crumbs and also help the retention of moisture by their sponge-like properties. For this reason, you should always dig in compost, manure or other organic matter before planting in order to ensure moist, fertile soil.

Many herbs require at least slightly alkaline conditions; to be more precise, they require a pH of above 7. The pH scale is a measure that runs from 0 to 14, and whereas soils with a pH above 7 are alkaline, those with a pH below 7 are called acid. Most soils lie naturally somewhere between about pH 6 and pH 7.5 (and are therefore more or less neutral) and most herbs will be happy in these kinds of conditions but distinctly unhappy if the soil is appreciably acid,

that is below a pH of about 5.0. The pH of a slightly acid soil can be raised fairly simply, however, by adding lime, and this procedure is well worth doing in the autumn before planting a new herb garden in the following spring.

Right: *Well-worn steps provide a welcome path through this abundant, tumbling herb garden.*
Left: *Gravel pathways weave through these low-growing flower and herb beds, with a striking array of chives, allium, forget-me-nots, sage, thyme and conifers.*

Design and Styles of Herb Gardens

Gardens are such personal creations that the best results are achieved when people design them for themselves, perhaps with reference to some professional pointers over practical pitfalls. So, by this token, you can plant a herb garden exactly as you wish and no one should criticize you for it.

Much of the interest in herb growing is an historical rather than a practical one, and much of early gardening was carried out for herbal reasons. Many of the methods of planting herbs that were developed over the years were extremely attractive and many people are drawn to the idea of a herb garden that mimics in some way these very traditional growing methods. Such a planting can fit very happily into an otherwise modern garden.

But before outlining how an historically inspired herb garden

Right: *Sage, thyme, oregano and tarragon look striking alongside a variety of grasses in this contemporary herb garden.*
Opposite: *Raised concrete beds house a combination of cotton lavender, thyme and cornflower.*

can be planned, let's just start with a very simple planting of herbs for someone who does, indeed, only want a small collection of herbs for use in the kitchen. They should be planted as close to the kitchen as possible, commensurate with the requirements for sun and soil (see page 9). It really is surprising how a few more metres to walk will deter busy cooks from making full use of the fresh herbs that are available. To grow a basic range of herbs for the kitchen (see the list on page 15) you will need an area of about 2 × 2m (7 × 7ft); ideally, 3 × 3m (10 × 10ft). Remember to plant the taller types at the back and then, most importantly, put in some stepping stones, for a herb garden is unlike an ornamental flower bed in that you will need to walk in and among the plants as you snip and collect. Without stepping stones, you will find you have compacted soil and muddy shoes – another inconvenience if you have just stepped out while in the middle of stirring a sauce. And that is all there is to it: easy to plant, easy to maintain.

And so now to the historically inspired herb garden and, be it medieval or Victorian in its inspiration, the watchword is formality. The design will be based on angles and symmetry. Measure accurately the area that you have available for planting and transfer the outline to a scale drawn on graph paper. Allowing for the smallest individual planting unit or bed of about 60 × 60cm (24 × 24in), examine ways in which the whole can attractively be divided up. Bear in mind always the need for access to all parts, even if not to pick and collect herbs, then for maintenance. Paths dividing up the discrete parts of the area could be of grass (hard to mow in confined space and also giving you a great deal of edge trimming); bricks (arranged in any number of patterns; time-consuming to do but visually superb although you must use durable types that won't crumble); or gravel (easy, cheap, very attractive but annoying and messy if you have to walk over it with muddy boots). Mortared pebbles and stone slabs are less effective as they are less formal; concrete or other modern slabs or blocks will look terrible unless they are very good copies of brick paviors.

If you have room and want a medieval or Tudor feel to the planting, then use edging plants around the beds. The best by far is the compact and common form of box, *Buxus sempervirens* 'Suffruticosa' (see page 284) although *Santolina* (page 230) and other plants are sometimes used as cheaper, short-term substitutes. If you are really ambitious, then the box could be planted in knot-garden fashion, the miniature hedges imitating the pattern of knotted ropes. In a design of this complexity, you must mark on your graph paper the precise position of each of the edging plants. Then with canes and twine,

mark out the actual area to be planted and, square by square, plant the herb garden, following the marked positions on your design very carefully.

Planting herbs in the gaps between the spokes of a wooden cartwheel laid on the ground is certainly a very simple way of creating attractive, formal planting in a small area. If you can't obtain a real cartwheel, then the pattern can be laid out, in whatever size you prefer, in bricks. Look at the designs in old gardening books (even ancient works have been reprinted in recent years) for your inspiration and think, also, of perhaps creating a themed garden – of aromatic herbs mentioned by Shakespeare, say, or of plants used to control fevers, of white-flowered herbs, of Chinese herbs; but above all, have fun with plants that are, by and large, easy to grow and steeped in historical and mythical interest.

Left: *The secret to this walled herb garden is variegated box interspersed with masses of herbs, including purple sage, tansy, fennel, monkshood, flowering alliums and aquilegias and pink bistort.*

Basic Herbs for the Kitchen

Plants and Planting

There are two main ways of buying new herb plants: by shopping personally at your local garden centre, or by obtaining them from a specialist herb nursery, which is likely to have a much wider range and to supply the plants by mail-order and online.

At a garden centre, the plants will be in small pots; mail-order plants and those ordered online these days may well be dispatched in small plastic modules, packed together in sophisticated and very ingenious packaging which ensures they can be sent safely and reliably. Although herb plants in containers may, in theory, be planted at all times of the year, they are, in general, much less robust than shrubs or herbaceous border perennials and so are best bought and planted in spring or autumn, the periods when mail-order and online suppliers tend to send out their stock.

As explained on page 18 most herbs, especially the shrubby types, aren't long-term plants. But this shouldn't mean that their planting positions are prepared any less thoroughly than long-lived plants.

They are generally fairly small, however, and for this reason, it's easier to prepare and plant a sizeable patch of the herb bed at a time, than to try the more time-consuming operation of making a precise planting position for each individual. It is worthwhile to double dig a herb bed in advance of planting, or at least to dig in compost (generally better than animal manures for herbs) to a good spade's depth.

Once you obtain your plants, from whatever source, plant them promptly so that they are able to establish without delay. The planting position should be prepared by digging a hole of approximately twice the volume of the pot ball of compost or about four times the volume if the plant is in a mailing module. The soil removed should be mixed with a roughly equal volume of compost or similar organic

matter and a handful of bone meal. This is rich in phosphate, which aids root development and will help the plant to establish quickly. In addition, always tease away the roots lightly around the edge of the compost ball as otherwise they tend to grow inwards, towards the more moist compost in the centre rather than out into the surrounding soil. Once the plant is in its planting hole, firm the soil carefully with your boot, or if it is a small plant, with the handle of your trowel as you fill the hole, but don't ram it down too hard. Ensure that you finish by making a small mound with the soil sloping away from the plant's stem. This will prevent water

from collecting at the base, and then freezing and causing damage. Finally, remember to water the plant well after planting.

Food and Water

Food and water are, of course, important for all garden plants although, as a group, herbs probably require less than many others. They are not generally grown for large and lush flowers or fruit which would necessitate a high level of potash. And although for the majority, it is the leaves that are harvested and used, too much nitrogen, which is generally advocated for leafy growth, can also be detrimental. High nitrogen feeds are fine for leafy plants like cabbages that grow relatively quickly, but with smaller-leaved and generally slower-growing herbs, it can result in soft, watery and rather tasteless foliage. Recommended, therefore, is a light dressing of a balanced general feed containing roughly equal percentages of nitrogen, phosphate and potash. Fish, blood and bone, containing a nitrogen (N), phosphate (P) and potassium (K) ratio of around 5:5:6, serves the purpose admirably.

Water is important, too, and the herb garden, with its sunny position and free-draining soil can often be a dry one. Apply a light organic mulch once or twice each year at times when the soil is damp. Almost any of the normal organic mulching materials can be used but, because herbs are usually small plants, the grosser materials like very coarse compost are best avoided; opt instead for fine compost or, best of all, well-rotted leaf mould.

After-care and Propagation

By and large, herbs aren't plants to be left undisturbed for long periods. Most of the herbaceous perennials soon become too large for their allotted space and most of the small shrubby types become leggy and unkempt after two or three years and require replacing.

There are also a few annual and biennial species that are obviously the most short-lived of all. So regular renewal of the plants is an important part of herb growing and while one option is simply to buy anew from your garden centre or nursery, it is much cheaper and much more

satisfying to propagate your own from your existing stock, provided the plants are healthy. Propagating from diseased plants will merely perpetuate any problems.

There are three main ways in which herbs may be propagated: from seed, by division, and by cuttings. Most

Above: Lavandula angustifolia *'Hidcote' cuttings covered with a pierced plastic bag.*

types of herb can be raised from seed; but many types, certainly of culinary herb, shouldn't be. This is because the best varieties do not come true from seed and so must be propagated vegetatively, by division or cuttings. Nonetheless, many medicinal herbs and, of course, the annuals and biennials among the kitchen types can and should be raised from seed and this may be done very easily. Seed can be sown either outdoors, in the final growing positions, or in a greenhouse or other protected place from which the plants must be hardened-off before being planted out.

Indoors

To sow seeds on the greenhouse bench or the kitchen window ledge, be sure to buy them fresh, packeted and branded from a reputable supplier. You will require a compost in which to sow them, a propagator, water, in most instances light and some means of supplying an adequate temperature. The compost should be a proprietary mixture, either soil-based or soilless but always use fresh for each batch of seeds.

There are many types of propagator and at their simplest, these need be no more than a plant pot and a plastic bag. In practice, small plant pots are ideal for herbs as you won't need many plants of each type. Several small pots can be stood inside a standard-size plastic seed tray covered with a purpose-made rigid plastic cover with adjustable vents. These are usually purchased complete with the seed tray base and the same device can also be used for striking cuttings. But whatever equipment you adopt, ensure that it is washed before being used again.

Generally, seeds require a slightly higher temperature in order to germinate than the plants will ever require again. Moreover, within fairly well-defined limits for each type of seed, the higher the temperature the more rapid and uniform the germination. Provision of an adequate and appropriate temperature is thus extremely important, but remember that it is the temperature of the compost, not the air above it, that really matters (what gardeners call 'bottom heat') and the best way to provide this is with a purpose-made sand bench containing an electric heating cable or a heating mat, on which the propagators are stood. Some models operate at low voltage so a wire may safely be run to the greenhouse from the house if you have no independent greenhouse electricity supply. Thermostatic control should enable you to regulate the heat fairly precisely but pay careful attention to the temperature recommendations given on the seed packet.

Once the seedlings are showing their green cotyledons (seed leaves) above the compost, open the vents on your propagator half-way. As the seedlings stand upright and elongate, the vents should be opened fully and when the first true leaves have expanded, the cover should then be removed. It's always very important to attend to watering carefully at this stage and to ensure that the seedlings are not exposed to direct hot sun. Sow two or three seeds to each pot, pull out the weaker seedlings if more than one emerges, and there will then be no need to prick them out. But you do need to harden them off.

The place to harden-off seedlings is the cold-frame, into which the pots of seedlings are placed. Always allow at least two weeks for hardening-off before planting out. In the first week, the frame cover is left half open in the daytime but closed up at night. In the second week, it is left fully open in the daytime and half open at night. If you do not have a cold-frame, the pots of seedlings may be put outside in the daytime and taken under cover at night, although this is laborious, and an inexpensive cold-frame makes a very worthwhile investment.

Outdoors

Gardeners talk of obtaining a good tilth before sowing seeds. Tilth is a curious, almost indefinable quality perhaps best summed up as the soil condition in which seeds will germinate and seedlings will grow most satisfactorily. This means, in practice, that the soil crumbs must be broken down finely enough for the tiny roots to be able to make fairly unimpeded progress while, at the same time, there must be enough pores between the crumbs to ensure that the roots are well furnished with water and air. The soil must also be uniform in its structure, and all of these attributes combine to ensure that it warms up evenly and quickly.

The sowing area should generally be roughly dug, and organic matter incorporated in the autumn, then left with fairly large clods over winter. By the spring, the winter rains and frost will have broken these down but the soil will still be in a lumpy and uneven state, and there will certainly be some weed growth. The soil should then be dug again, using a fork rather than a spade, the weeds removed and the large lumps broken down with the back of the fork. This operation can be performed as soon as the soil begins to dry out in the spring – the precise timing will obviously vary according to your local conditions and with the nature of your soil; as mentioned on page 9, a sandy soil will be in a workable condition much sooner than a clay one. About one week before sowing, the area should be raked to remove any remaining large clods and, at the same time, a balanced general

Right: *Herbs in pots ready for sowing. Left to right: rosemary, oregano and sage.*

fertilizer should be scattered over the soil and thus incorporated into the first upper few centimetres. Rake alternately in directions at 90 degrees to each other in order to obtain as level a surface as possible.

On the whole, herb seeds are best broadcast sown; that is, scattered in small groups rather than straight lines, and discrete areas within the herb garden should be prepared for them, the soil being carefully raked away for sowing and then raked back again afterwards and carefully firmed. But always sow sparingly and, if necessary, thin out the seedlings to the spacing recommended on the packet if too many emerge.

Division

As the old, but true, gardening adage says, division is the simplest method of multiplication. Large clumps of herbaceous perennials can be pulled apart and the smaller pieces replanted. The best times of year to do this are autumn or early spring and the procedure is straightforward enough. Dig up the mature clump with a fork and pull it first into two, then more pieces. If possible, do this by hand, but if not, by inserting two forks, back to

back, and levering them apart. Never use a spade as this is very likely to sever and damage the roots. From a clump of about 15cm (6in) diameter, it should be possible to obtain approximately 10 new plants but always tear off and discard those parts that lay in the centre of the original crown, as these will degenerate and never give rise to any vigorous new growth.

Below: *Propagation of rosemary plants – dipping cuttings in rooting powder.*

Cuttings

There are three main types of cutting: softwood, semi-ripe and hardwood. The names are self-explanatory and reflect the time in the season when each should be taken – softwood early on in the growing cycle, and hardwood at the end. Although it is hardly ever essential, hormone rooting powder may be used with all cuttings but it is most beneficial with softwood types.

With the exception of hardwood cuttings, all types should be rooted (or 'struck') in a covered chamber, either a propagator of the type used for seed growing, or a covered cold-frame. It is very important to maintain a moist atmosphere around the cuttings since they will otherwise lose water through their leaves at a time when, lacking roots, they are unable to replace it from below. Even with a covered propagator, therefore, you should pay careful attention to the moisture content of the rooting medium and use a hand sprayer to mist over the cuttings regularly. The cold-frame can also be used for hardwood cuttings, although you can also root these in a sheltered spot in the garden, inserting the shoots in a narrow 'V'-shaped trench in the bottom with a layer of sand sprinkled in the bottom. The type of medium (sand, soil-based compost and so forth) into which the cuttings are placed varies with the type of plant and suggestions of which to use are in the individual herb descriptions.

In general, cuttings should be removed from the parent plant with a clean cut made just below a bud. Evergreen shrubby herbs, such as sweet bay, can present problems; even if cuttings are taken during their dormant season in the conventional hardwood manner, the presence of leaves means that water will still be lost at a time when the plant has no means of replacing it. The difficulty can often be overcome by layering – the process where a stem is anchored into the soil while it is still attached to the parent plant. The disadvantage is that some patience is needed, as layerings rarely root satisfactorily in less than 18 months.

Herbs in Containers

It should come as no surprise that herbs can be grown in containers, for most types of plant can. The advantage of growing them in this way is that even people with very tiny gardens can have a small collection of useful herbs on a paved area or path edge. Also, an even smaller collection can be maintained on an indoor windowsill or in the house during winter when outdoor plants have died down.

Always use a soil-based compost and ornamental terracotta pots are a good choice, because they look so appropriate and because they allow the compost to breathe and are much less likely to encourage the root rotting that can happen so easily in plastic pots. Be sure that the containers have adequate drainage holes and don't allow them to stand in saucers of water. Plenty of water and free

Left: Coreopsis, Thymus, Salvia, Helichrysum italicum *and* Ocimum *in windowbox on garden fence.*
Right: *Containers of lavender on small garden patio.*

drainage are essential for successful herb growing. Choose a pot of appropriate size to the vigour of each type of plant (details of plant sizes are given in the individual descriptions), and keep one pot for each type of herb. Although a mixed planting of different herbs might look attractive initially, their varying growth rates will make for problems.

The only pot sold specifically for herb use is the so-called parsley pot, a tall pot with holes in the side through which the plants emerge. Well planted, they look extremely attractive but there is a trick to planting them. If you completely fill the pot with compost and then try to push in the plants through the holes, you will damage the roots and they will be unlikely to establish satisfactorily. The secret is to put in compost only up to the level of the first holes and then carefully push the plants through the holes from the inside, then add more compost up to the next holes and so on until the pot is full.

Experiment with your container growing; plant some herbs in hanging baskets and window boxes (pot them up individually within the window box so any that fade or require replacing may readily be replaced), and group together containers of different sizes. Always be sure to place containers in a warm and sunny position, don't neglect watering during the summer and be prepared, especially with large and vigorous plants, to give a little extra feed in the form of a balanced liquid fertilizer once or twice during the growing season.

There are a few rather special uses of containers that are mentioned in the individual descriptions of each herb. These are for very vigorous plants, such as mint, that would otherwise, very quickly, take over an entire herb garden. As suggested on page 176, the solution is to grow such herbs in containers and sink the entire container to rim level in the soil.

Picking and Preserving Herbs

The best way to use herbs is to pick them fresh from the garden. Just as with vegetables and salad greens, this is the great advantage of growing your own rather than relying on the shop-bought product. But even with the seasonal extension you can achieve by growing small herbs indoors in pots, it just isn't possible to have everything fresh all year round. For medicinal use, moreover, some type of preparation is almost always necessary.

As explained earlier, this is a gardening, not a cookbook or medicinal book, and so makes no attempt to venture into the intricate details of using herbs for either purpose. The following guidelines for picking and preserving culinary herbs especially, however, should be helpful.

Take care not to eat or preserve herbs that have been sprayed with any chemical and, however they are to be treated, those for preserving should always be picked fresh. Dried or frozen herbs are never as good as lush, fresh herbs; but even dried or frozen herbs are better than brown or yellow herbs. The leaves of annual or deciduous types should be picked while they are young, which will generally mean in the early part of summer. They may be picked from evergreen species at any time of the year, although the fresh new leaves are usually preferable. It's thought that leaves are best picked in the early morning before the heat of the day causes their volatile chemical components to evaporate and dilute.

Flowers are best picked just before they open fully, and fruits and seeds when they are fully ripe, but before they fall or are shed. This will probably mean watching and testing them over a period of weeks, cutting off the seedheads carefully, tying bags over them and then hanging them up in a warm, well ventilated place to complete the drying process.

Although the traditional way of preserving herbs is to dry them, there is no denying that the flavour is considerably inferior to that of the fresh product. For those herbs that it does remain the best or only method, a microwave oven can be used for drying, though some herbalists claim that the more subtle flavours and properties are lost. Freezing is an excellent technique for preserving herbs of most kinds; certainly delicate

Above: *Garlic is easy to grow and, historically, has been cultivated for both culinary and medical uses.*
Left: *Harvesting parsley.*

types, such as parsley, really do freeze well. There is so little to the operation that there is absolutely no excuse for not freezing some of your favourite summer herbs for winter use when very little is available fresh from the garden: simply put the herbs in small batches in plastic freezer bags and freeze. And of course, other, less common methods of preservation are appropriate to particular types of herb – in oil, in herb vinegar, sugared and crystallized, and in pickles.

Pests and Diseases

Herbs are probably no more or less prone to pest and disease problems than any other type of garden plant, although the fact that most are not grown principally for their flowers (which also tend to be small) means that flower problems are perhaps less significant. And although the leaves of many are used in culinary or medicinal applications, it generally matters little if the odd hole happens to be present.

Nonetheless, the same overall principles apply to herbs as to any other garden plants: prevention is better than cure but there are limits to how reliable it can be. There are chemical and non-chemical ways of combating problems, not always of equal effectiveness but the decision on how important a particular problem is and how much damage is tolerable is very much a personal one.

There is, however, an additional factor to bear in mind in relation to control measures. It is preferable not to use chemicals at all on edible plants, but since this is not always possible, this sections suggests only those products that could be considered the safest in respect of the minimum period that must elapse

from the procedures you will be used to with chemicals so read the manufacturers' directions carefully.

The tables on pages 30–33 give a simple key to symptoms to enable you to identify easily the most common problems that may be encountered in the herb garden, together with a summary of recommended control measures and details of the various chemicals available.

Above: *Mint rust.*
Left: *Flea beetle damage on* Eruca vesicaria.
Right: *Willow carrot aphids (*Cavariella aegopodii*) on parsley.*

between application and use of the plants. Wherever the option exists, moreover, biological control measures are suggested, an increasing number of which are being made available to the amateur gardener. So far, those of relevance to the herb garden are two different systems based on beneficial nematodes (eel-worms), one of which attacks the larvae of the vine weevil and the other, slugs. The methods of using the nematode techniques, in particular, will be rather different

SYMPTOMS ON LEAVES

PROBLEM	DETAIL	PROBABLE CAUSE
Wilting	General	Short of water • Root pests or disease • Wilt disease
Holed	Generally ragged	Small pests (millipedes, woodlice) • Capsid bugs
	Elongated holes; usually with slime present	Slugs or snails
	Fairly large holes over entire leaf or confined to edges	Caterpillars • Beetles
Discoloured	Black	Sooty mould
	Predominantly red	Short of water
	More or less bleached	Fertilizer deficiency • Short of water • Too much water
	Irregular yellowish patterns	Virus
	Irregular tunnels	Leaf miners
	Surface flecking	Leafhoppers
	Brown (scorched) in spring	Frost
Spotted	Brownish, irregular, no mould	Leaf spot
	Small, dusty, brown, black or bright yellow-orange coloured	Rust
Mouldy	Black	Sooty mould
	Grey, fluffy	Grey mould
	White (or rarely brown), velvety	Mildew
Infested with insects	White, moth-like, tiny	Whiteflies
	Green, grey, black or other colour	Aphids
	Flat, encrusted, like limpets	Scale insects
	Large, six legs, worm-like	Caterpillars
Cobwebs present	Leaves also discoloured	Red spider mites

SYMPTOMS ON FLOWERS

Drooping	General	Short of water • End of flowering period
Tattered	Masses of tiny holes	Caterpillars
	Large pieces torn away	Birds

PROBLEM	DETAIL	PROBABLE CAUSE
Removed entirely	Usually discarded nearby	Birds
Discoloured	Powdery white covering	Mildew
Mouldy	Fluffy grey mould	Grey mould

SYMPTOMS ON STEMS OR BRANCHES

Eaten through	On young plants	Slugs or snails
	On older plants	Mice, voles, rabbits
Infested with insects	Green, grey, black or other colour	Aphids
	Flat, encrusted like limpets	Scale insects
	Large, six legs, worm-like	Caterpillars
Rotten	At base, young plants	Stem and foot rot
	On shrubby herbs	Decay fungus
Dying back	General	Short of water • Coral spot • Root pest or disease

SOME FUNGICIDES, INSECTICIDES AND PESTICIDAL CHEMICALS USEFUL FOR CONTROLLING PROBLEMS ON HERBS

FUNGICIDES	USES AND COMMENTS
Tebuconazole	Systemic, especially useful for leaf spots and rust
Triticonazole	Systemic, especially useful for leaf spots and rust
Sulfur and fatty acids*	Non-systemic, many foliage diseases

INSECTICIDES	USES AND COMMENTS
Natural soaps*	Contact, most pests
Synthetic pyrethroids	Contact, most pests

FUNGICIDES	USES AND COMMENTS
Pyrethrum*	Contact, most pests

SLUG AND SNAIL KILLERS	USES AND COMMENTS
Ferric phosphate	As pellets
Metaldehyde	As pellets, mini-pellets or liquid

TREATMENTS FOR COMMON PEST AND DISEASE PROBLEMS ON HERBS

PROBLEM	TREATMENT
Aphids	Use a proprietary contact insecticide; pick off affected shoots by hand or wash off insects with a hose
Beetles	Normally, treatment is not necessary or justified but in cases of extensive attack use a proprietary contact insecticide
Birds	Erect netting or other protection; in really severe cases, erect bird scarers but remember that all birds enjoy legal protection and may not be harmed
Capsid bugs	The insects are too unpredictable and erratic in occurrence to make any treatment feasible
Caterpillars	Pick off by hand if the caterpillars can be found and are present in small numbers. If masses of insects occur, pick off and destroy entire affected leaves
Coral spot	Cut away and destroy affected branches or twigs, cutting well into the healthy wood
Fertilizer deficiency	Give general balanced liquid fertilizer
Fungal decay	Destroy affected parts or entire plants; no other treatment is feasible
Grey mould	Destroy affected parts
Leaf hopper	The insects are too erratic and unpredictable to make any treatment feasible
Leaf miner	Remove and destroy affected leaves
Leaf spot	In most instances no treatment is necessary for leaf spot diseases are rarely severe. Where attacks appear to be related to general poor growth however, replace plants
Mice	Set traps or use proprietary poison
Mildew	Ensure that plants are not allowed to become too dry and apply systemic fungicide or sulfur
Millipedes	Clear away debris where they congregate
Rabbits	The only sure protection is to erect a wire netting fence with the lower edge turned outwards at 90 degrees over the soil surface
Red spider	No treatment is really feasible although keeping plants well watered and mulched will help limit the impact of attacks
Root pests	Normally, no treatment is feasible but for vine weevil, use biological control (see page 29)

PROBLEM	TREATMENT
Root disease	Destroy severely affected plants
Rust	No treatment possible on edible herbs; spray others with triticonazole or tebucanazole fungicide
Scale insects	Spray or drench with systemic insecticide
Slugs	Use proprietary slug pellets or liquid controls such as traps baited with beer. Surround the base of plants with fine powders such as ash or soot or a low barrier of finely spiny twigs such as gorse
Snails	If serious, use methods recommended for slugs but generally they are less serious and fewer in number, and can be combated by collecting them by hand and by locating and eradicating them from their hiding places
Sooty mould	Wash off mould with water or destroy badly affected leaves and then identify and treat the insect pest responsible for the honeydew on which the mould grows
Stem and foot rot	Little can be done but as it is often associated with waterlogging, improve drainage of the affected area
Virus	Effects are usually mild, so no treatment is necessary
Voles	Set mouse traps or use proprietary poison baits
Whiteflies	No treatment is feasible on outdoor plants
Woodlice	Locate and eradicate pests from hiding places

* Generally acceptable
to organic gardeners

NB: It should be noted that some of these chemicals are only available in particular formulations or in combination with certain other chemicals. Some may also be marketed for specific pest or disease problems only. In every case, you must read the label directions carefully to be sure that the product is being used for the purpose and in the manner for which it is intended. The names given in this chart are those of the active chemical ingredients. These will not be the same as the product names but will be found printed on the product label. See also the comments on page 26 concerning the use of chemicals on edible plants.

HERB DIRECTORY

Achillea millefolium

Yarrow

There are also cultivated border varieties of this herbaceous perennial in colours that are not appealing to all but, nonetheless, if yarrow is grown in an unaltered form in the herb garden, its silver-tinted and very finely divided, almost feathery foliage (hence *millefolium* – thousand leaves) has its attractions.

Cultivation and Care

Mulch lightly in autumn and spring, and give a light dressing of a balanced general fertilizer in spring. Cut back dead flower heads or alternatively cut while the plant is in flower and then dry these flower heads for ornamental use. Propagation of the plant is by means of division in spring or by seed sown in a light, soil-based compost in an unheated propagator in the late spring.

Left: *White yarrow.*

Right: *Herbal tea with* Achillea.

Yarrow Basics

Problems: None.

Recommended Varieties: Normal species only is available as a herb.

Ornamental Appeal: Feathery, silvery-grey foliage and a head of small white, daisy-like flowers in summer. Some of the border forms have flower heads of other colours.

Site and Soil: Full sun to very light shade, most soils including fairly dry and poor sites but best in good, rich, well drained loams.

Hardiness: Very hardy, tolerating −20°C (−4°F) or below.

Size: Varies greatly with soil conditions; on a good site, will attain about 75 × 45cm (30 × 18in) after three years.

Yarrow Uses

Culinary Flowers, either whole or as individual florets, are used in salads and also cooked dishes including cheese recipes, soups and omelettes. Leaves are also used in salads.

Non-Culinary Various extracts, as well as the raw leaves, have been used to make healing preparations on skin bruises and wounds.

Acorus calamus

Sweet Flag

An herbaceous rhizomatous perennial, this imposing species is one of the very few common water plants that possess herbal properties and as such is well worth cultivating in larger gardens as a pond marginal. In common with so many other water-garden species, it is a member of the Arum family, despite the superficial resemblance of its foliage to that of irises. In 'flag' it even shares one of their common names but it is the 'sweet' part of this species' name that earns it an entry here, for the bruised or broken leaves certainly do have an appealing, sweet and extraordinarily spicy fragrance.

Cultivation and Care

Cut down dead foliage and flower stems in autumn or, in cold areas, in the spring. Propagate by division in the spring.

Sweet Flag Basics

Problems: None.

Recommended Varieties: The normal species is the usual herb plant although the variety 'Argenteostriatus', with cream and golden leaf stripes is neater and slower growing.

Above: Acorus calamus (*Sweet Flag*) *cut up rhizome.*
Left: Acorus calamus flower spike.

Ornamental Appeal: Iris-like leaves, tiny green-brown flowers in arum-like spikes towards tops of stems in summer.

Site and Soil: Full sun or very light shade as water garden marginal in water up to 25cm (10in) deep.

Hardiness: Very hardy, tolerating −20°C (−4°F) or below.

Size: Will attain about 1.2m × 75cm (4ft × 30in) after four or five years.

Sweet Flag Uses

Culinary Little in present day cooking but in the past the rhizomes were used to flavour meat.

Non-Culinary Dried leaves or rhizomes for potpourri, the leaves were once used as an aromatic floor covering, and a drug to treat intestinal, kidney and gall-bladder problems (among others) is extracted from the rhizomes.

Agastache foeniculum

Anise Hyssop

This herbaceous perennial is one of the lesser known herbs in the family Lamiaceae. It is North American and, unlike its relatives, it is a recent plant in European herb gardens, having been introduced only in the early 19th century. It is an attractive, characteristic labiate with a neater clump-forming habit than many, that can easily be grown as a half-hardy perennial in colder areas.

Cultivation and Care

In milder areas, mulch lightly in the autumn and spring and give a light dressing of balanced general fertilizer in spring. Cut back top growth in spring and propagate by division in spring. In cooler areas, take semi-ripe cuttings in summer for overwintering in a cold greenhouse and discard old plants or pot up and keep as stock under cover. The plant tends to be fairly short lived and, even in mild regions, stock should be renewed from cuttings every three years. It can also be raised from seed sown in early summer in an unheated propagator in soil-based compost.

Left: Agastache foeniculum *in bloom.*
Right: *Herbal tea made of* Agastache anisata.

Anise Hyssop Basics

Problems: Mildew in hot summers.

Recommended Varieties: Normal species is usually available although the rather attractive white-flowered varieties 'Alabaster' and 'Alba' will sometimes be seen. A related species, the so-called Korean Mint, *Agastache rugosa*, is also sometimes offered.

Ornamental Appeal: Typically labiate, nettle-shaped leaves, spikes of small purplish-blue flowers from about mid-summer onwards.

Site and Soil: Full sun to very light shade with shelter from cold winds, in light, free-draining but fairly rich soil.

Hardiness: Moderately hardy, tolerating about −10°C (14°F).

Size: It will grow to attain about 50–75 × 45cm (20–30 × 18in) after three years.

Anise Hyssop Uses

Culinary Dried leaves can be used as a pleasing aniseed-flavoured infusion.
Non-Culinary None.

Agrimonia eupatoria

Agrimony

Grown purely as a border ornamental, agrimony is a bit of a disappointment and, in truth, it is rather a feeble-looking thing. It produces very slender spikes of tiny, star-like yellow flowers during the summer but the drawback is that not only are the stems so

slender, but also that rather few of the flowers are ever in bloom at the same time. Nonetheless, this herbaceous perennial is a good plant for attracting bees, it has a sweet perfume (at least, if you can get your nose close enough), and has a long enough history of herbal use to justify its inclusion in a collection.

Cultivation and Care

Mulch lightly in the autumn and spring and give a light dressing of a balanced fertilizer in spring. Cut back dead flower heads or alternatively cut while in flower and dry to make a honey-scented potpourri. Propagate by division in spring or autumn or by seed sown in a light, soil-based compost in an unheated propagator in the spring.

Agrimony Basics

Problems: None.

Recommended Varieties: Normal species only is available.

Ornamental Appeal: Spikes of small, yellow flowers in summer. Divided leaves, rather reminiscent of meadowsweet, to which it is related.

Left: Agrimonia eupatoria.
Below: Agrimonia eupatoria *tea*.

Site and Soil: Full sun, in a wide range of soils provided they are fairly light and well drained.

Hardiness: Very hardy, tolerating −20°C (−4°F) or below.

Size: Will attain 1– 1.2m × 30cm (3– 4ft × 12in) after about three or four years.

Agrimony Uses

Culinary None.

Non-Culinary A sweet-scented herbal tea can be made from the leaves and infusions for sore throats, coughs and other complaints. Also yields a yellow dye.

Ajuga reptans

Bugle

Bugle can be used as a striking, ground-cover species for shady places. Such a degree of shade tolerance is a considerable virtue in any herb plant, most of which are sun lovers. The deep purple leaves of the best forms contrast superbly with the rich blue flowers in early summer but many people find this herbaceous perennial too invasive and too mildew prone, and for these reasons it cannot really be considered a true gardening classic.

Cultivation and Care

Mulch in autumn and spring until well established and give a light dressing of a balanced general fertilizer in spring. Cut back dead flower heads for tidiness and also if mildew sets in. Propagate by division in spring or autumn or by removal of naturally rooted runners.

Bugle Basics

Problems: Mildew.

Recommended Varieties: Normal species has green leaves and mid-blue flowers; there are also many varieties but among the more attractive (although no more valuable as herbs) are 'Alba' (white flowers), 'Atropurpurea' (dark purple leaves, dark blue-purple flowers) and 'Burgundy Glow' (leaves slightly variegated, deep red and green).

Above: Ajuga reptans.
Left: Ajuga reptans *in bloom*.

Ornamental Appeal: Short spikes of typically labiate flowers in white, or shades of blue and purple. Variously coloured, more or less oval leaves, ground-covering habit.

Site and Soil: Full sun to deep shade but more mildew prone in the sun; in most soils but grows best in fairly rich, organic sites.

Hardiness: Very hardy, tolerating at least −20°C (−4°F) or below.

Size: Will attain about 15cm × 1m (6in × 3ft) after about four or five years.

Bugle Uses

Culinary None.

Non-Culinary Several, including lowering blood pressure, the treatment of bruises and other blood problems.

Alchemilla mollis

Lady's Mantle

Alchemilla is high on the list of indispensable garden plants, whether herbal or not. A perennial, it really is among the best and most adaptable herbaceous ground cover but it also has a long and interesting history as a herb. The drops of rain or dew that form, mercury-like, on the foliage were once considered to have magical properties while the 'Lady' of the name is the Virgin Mary, although, coincidentally, many of its medicinal uses were gynaecological. If there is a drawback, it is that it is a bit too successful as ground cover in small gardens although there is a related, less-vigorous, alternative species.

Cultivation and Care

Cut back dead foliage in late autumn and mulch, then mulch again in early spring and give a balanced general fertilizer. Trim back flower heads as they fade and turn brown. Propagate by division in spring or autumn or by removal of self-sown seedlings.

Lady's Mantle Basics

Problems: None.

Left: *Lady's mantle (Alchemilla mollis).*
Right: *Lady's mantle herbal therapy.*

Recommended Varieties: Many plants once called *Alchemilla mollis* or *Alchemilla vulgaris* are now considered to be separate species, but the two forms most generally useful in the herb garden (and sharing herbal properties) are the true *A. mollis* and the less vigorous, *A. alpina*, which is a good plant for confined space.

Ornamental Appeal: More or less rounded, toothed, light green leaves with feathery heads of yellow-green flowers in early summer. Leaves of *A. alpina* are more strongly divided and finger-like.

Site and Soil: Full sun to moderate shade, in most soils but intolerant of very heavy and cold conditions and best on slightly alkaline sites.

Hardiness: Very hardy, tolerating −20°C (−4°F) or below.

Size: The true *A. mollis* will attain about 50 × 50cm (20 × 20in) after three years; *A. alpina* about half this.

Lady's Mantle Uses

Culinary Young leaves in small amounts may be added to salads to add a touch of bitterness.

Non-Culinary Several medicinal uses for gynaecological disorders, also as a treatment for skin complaints and as a wound healer.

45

Alliaria petiolata

Jack-by-the-Hedge, Garlic Mustard

Allaria is well known for being the food of the caterpillars of *Anthocharis cardamines*, the orange-tip butterfly, and both are a welcome sight in early spring. So-called because it is often found growing in the margins of hedges, Jack-by-the-hedge is a worthy herb plant and one that is sadly under appreciated. It is one of the oldest used for culinary purposes and is distinctive for the garlic-like smell the leaves give off when crushed.

Cultivation and Care

Although it may be a short-lived perennial, it is probably best grown as a biennial; sow the seed initially in pots in spring for planting out in autumn and then allow it to self-seed. Cut down in late summer.

Right: Alliaria petiolata *(garlic mustard) being prepared for use in a salad.*
Left: *Fresh garlic mustard.*

Jack-by-the-Hedge Basics

Problems: None.

Recommended Varieties: Normal species only is available.

Ornamental Appeal: Spikes of rather short-lived white flowers in the early spring, and broad, more or less heart-shaped leaves.

Site and Soil: Light to moderate shade, in most soils, tolerant of fairly high moisture.

Hardiness: Very hardy, tolerating −20°C (−4°F) or below.

Size: Will attain about 75cm– 1m × 25cm (30in– 3ft × 10in) by its second year.

Jack-by-the-Hedge Uses

Culinary Chopped leaves make a tangy, slightly onion- or garlic-like addition to salads (the name *Alliaria* has the same origin as *Allium*), also cooked in various ways, and generally to impart flavour to sauces.

Non-Culinary Few medicinal, probably none still used.

Allium spp.

Herb Onions

This large and interesting genus has members that play a role in the kitchen and/or are interesting plants in their own right. Some have medicinal value and several are of good ornamental value, too. The genus *Allium*, of course, is a bulbous one and it is the bulb of the onion itself and some of the other species that is eaten, so the plants are grown as annuals. But for others, it is the foliage and flowers that are used and so these types can be grown as true perennials.

Cultivation and Care

All of the herb onions are best bought as plants. The old top growth should be cut down to soil level in autumn, the plants mulched lightly then and again in spring when they should also be given a light dressing of some balanced general fertilizer. Propagate by division in spring or autumn or by the removal and planting of the stem bulbils.

Herb Onion Basics

Problems: Rust (especially on chives), mildew, onion flies, white rot.

Right: Allium tuberosum *(Chinese chives).*
Opposite: *Chopped chives.*

Recommended Varieties: There are a number of closely related *Allium* species, most of which originate from eastern Europe and western Asia although several garden forms are unknown in the wild state. The onion (both bulb and salad or 'spring onion/scallion' varieties) and the multi-bulbed shallot are forms of *A. cepa*, but there is an intriguing herb-garden variety of this species called *Proliferum*, the tree or Egyptian onion, with large, shallot-sized bulbils produced at the stem tips among the flowers of inflorescence.

A. sativum is garlic, which tends to be grown solely for its clustered bulbs or 'cloves' but which does have perfectly edible foliage too and, in many areas, may be left to overwinter in the ground as a perennial.

A. scorodoprasum is the giant garlic or rocambole, which has a milder flavour and produces edible stem tip bulbils.

A. schoenoprasum is chives, the most familiar and useful herb onion, which produces little if any bulb and is grown solely for its foliage although the flowers are edible too.

A. tuberosum is Chinese chives, with a tuberous rather than bulbous root, flat, leek-like leaves, white flowers and a mild garlic flavour.

A. fistulosum is the Welsh or bunching onion, and although a vegetable rather than a herb species, it is worth mentioning as it too may be grown as a perennial because it produces a mass of onions at soil level for harvesting throughout the year.

Ornamental Appeal: Fresh green leaves and stems topped by usually spherical heads of mauve or white flowers. The chives especially are very attractive plants, while the tree onion has an undeniable appeal in its oddness.

Left: Allium schoenoprasum *(chives)*.
Right: Allium sativum *(garlic cloves)*.

Site and Soil: Full sun to very light shade; rich, organic but well drained soil will produce the best plant but most alliums will tolerate poorer soils too, although all resent heavy, waterlogged conditions.

Hardiness: Very hardy, tolerating −20°C (−4°F) or below.

Size: Varies considerably with species and variety from about 25 × 10cm (10 × 4in) for chives to 1m × 20–30cm (3ft × 8–12in) after two or three years for the tree onions.

Herb Onion Uses

Culinary Chopped leaves can be used as a more or less strongly flavoured addition (depending on the species) to salads, soups and cooked dishes. Bulbs or bulbils, whole or chopped, cooked or raw, are used in the same manner as onions. Flowers are edible also and have a milder flavour than bulbs or leaves; they make attractive additions to salads and as other garnishes.

Non-Culinary Most alliums, particularly garlic, are recognized for their antibiotic properties and many people eat garlic regularly to ward off colds. It is also widely used for its capacity to reduce blood cholesterol levels.

Aloe vera

Aloe Vera

We are more likely to think of *Aloe vera* in terms of jars of cream to be found in the bathroom cupboard than of plants to grow in your garden. Yet the herbaceous perennial *Aloe vera* is real enough and one of a huge genus of succulent members of the lily family. Perhaps even more surprising, for a plant that hails from the Mediterranean and similarly warm climates, is that it is a tolerably hardy species, although it is best grown in a container that can be moved into some form of shelter if harsh conditions prevail.

Cultivation and Care

Best if not mulched as this may give rise to crown-rotting. Water regularly during the summer but allow to dry out between waterings and give liquid fertilizer monthly. In colder areas, move under cover over winter. Propagate by removal of off-sets.

Aloe Vera Basics

Problems: Aphids, scale insects, mealybugs.

Right: *Aloe vera.*
Opposite: *Sap from fresh Aloe vera leaves.*

Recommended Varieties: Normal species only is available, but be warned that many other *Aloe* species are sold and grown as ornamentals. Some contain astringent sap, very different from that of *A. vera*.

Ornamental Appeal: Rosette of tapering, toothed, thick, fleshy, typically succulent, light green leaves, occasionally with a spike of very slender, trumpet-shaped, attractive yellow-orange flowers.

Site and Soil: Full sun, sheltered from cold winds, in free-draining, fertile soil, low in organic matter. In pots, in a good quality soil-based potting compost.

Hardiness: Fairly to moderately hardy, tolerating about −10°C (14°F).

Size: Will attain about 30 × 30cm (12 × 12in) within five years.

Aloe Vera Uses

Culinary None.

Non-Culinary As the basis of skin creams. The sap, when fresh, is applied and used to soothe and heal burned or otherwise damaged skin, but do take heed of the warning under the Recommended Varieties.

Aloysia citrodora

Lemon Verbena

This isn't the only herb with a strong lemon or citrus scent, but it is probably the one with the strongest. A shrubby perennial, it is native to warm areas of South America but has been grown in Europe for

around 200 years as a source of fragrant oil. Although it belongs to the same family as the ornamental verbena of many a summer hanging-basket, it is in a different genus and is certainly a less ornamental plant.

Cultivation and Care

Mulch in the autumn to protect from winter frost, and then again in spring. Give a balanced general fertilizer in spring and cut out any frost-damaged shoots. May also be fan-trained on a wall in the milder areas when the warmth reflected from the wall brings out the strong perfume. In cooler regions, grow in containers and then move under cover of a cold greenhouse in winter. Propagate by

Left: *Lemon verbena (*Aloysia citrodora*).*
Right: *Lemon verbena herbal tea.*

Lemon Verbena Uses

Culinary Leaves may be used for a herbal tea and also chopped to add lemon flavour to desserts and confectionery.

Non-Culinary Numerous medical applications, especially in infusions, also as the basis of skin creams and, predictably, in potpourri.

softwood cuttings in early summer in a covered propagator with some slight bottom heat.

Lemon Verbena Basics

Problems: None.

Recommended Varieties: Normal species only is available.

Ornamental Appeal: Fairly slight, small, pale, reddish flowers in loose spikes in late summer, and elongated, dark green leaves.

Site and Soil: Full sun, sheltered from cold winds, in free-draining, fertile soil, preferably slightly alkaline. In pots, in a good-quality, soil-based potting compost.

Hardiness: Fairly to moderately hardy, tolerating about −10°C (14°F).

Size: Varies considerably with site; in mild areas, will attain about 3 × 2m (10 × 7ft) within five years; in cooler areas, perhaps one-third of this.

Althaea officinalis
Marsh Mallow

Probably the first thing that comes to mind for most people when you say the name marshmallow is a sweet, rather sticky confection. Very few would know that it obtained its name, and originally, its stickiness and sweetness from a species of the mallow that happens to grow in marshes. Today, marshmallows, the confection, are made from other ingredients but the plant remains an interesting addition to a herb garden collection. In reality, salt marshes are its natural home but it is an adaptable plant and will grow in a wide range of soil types.

Cultivation and Care
Mulch in autumn and spring and give a light dressing of balanced general fertilizer in the spring. Cut down in autumn. Propagate by division in autumn or spring or by seed, sown in spring in a soil-based compost. An herbaceous perennial, it may also be grown quite successfully as a biennial.

Marsh Mallow Basics
Problems: None.

Recommended Varieties: Normal species only is available.

Right: *Root of marsh mallow.*
Left: Althaea officinalis *(marsh mallow).*

Ornamental Appeal: Moderate interest only; spikes of rather dull, velvety leaves with pale pink, typical mallow flowers borne in the axils.

Site and Soil: Full sun, in most soils provided they are fairly moist.

Hardiness: Very hardy, tolerating −20°C (−4°F) or below.

Size: Will attain about 2m × 50cm (7ft × 20in) within three years.

Marsh Mallow Uses

Culinary Chopped leaves and flowers can be used as a rather sweet addition to salads. Leaves may also be lightly boiled and steamed as a vegetable and roots par-boiled, then chopped and fried.

Non-Culinary Numerous uses, including infusions for coughs and sore throats and also to reduce external inflammation.

Anchusa officinalis

Bugloss, Alkanet

Not to be confused with viper's bugloss (see page 110) nor with bugle (see page 42), this is an herbaceous perennial with an old use revealed by its alternative name of alkanet, derived from an ancient Arabic word for henna. It was commonly grown as a source of the red henna dye, although, to confuse matters, henna was also obtained from

other boraginaceous plants, also known as alkanets. Its appearance is rather typical of many of its family in that it is a very predictable, uninspiring and rather unexciting plant.

Cultivation and Care

Mulch in autumn and spring and give a light dressing of balanced general fertilizer in the spring. Cut down in autumn. Propagate by division in autumn or spring or by seed, sown in spring in a soil-based compost. May also be grown quite successfully as a biennial.

Left: *Common bugloss or alkanet (*Anchusa officinalis*) in the meadow.*
Right: Anchusa officinalis.

Bugloss Basics

Problems: None.

Recommended Varieties: Normal species only is available.

Ornamental Appeal: Small purplish-blue flowers in characteristic, curling spikes, leaves narrowly elongated and, unlike many bristly members of the family, these are rather softly hairy.

Site and Soil: Best in full sun and on rather light, free-draining soils; unlikely to succeed on very wet or cold sites.

Hardiness: Very hardy, tolerating −20°C (−4°F) or below.

Size: Will attain about 1m × 50cm (3ft × 20in) within about two years.

Bugloss Uses

Culinary Chopped leaves and flowers can be used as an addition to salads.

Non-Culinary Apart from a source of dye, extracts of the roots have been put to various medicinal uses.

Anethum graveolens

Dill

Dill can be one of the trickiest and most frustrating of the common umbelliferous herbs if conditions aren't right, as it thrives best in warmer climates. Although a biennial, it is almost always grown as an annual and it is probably best known as a flavouring for the popular jars of pickled cucumbers and as a garnish for fish dishes. If all else fails, then fennel (see page 124) is a stronger-flavoured but definitely much easier substitute.

Cultivation and Care

Grow as a half-hardy annual, sowing seed in growing positions in spring and thinning to 30cm (12in) between plants. If more than one row is needed, space rows 60cm (24in) apart. The best plan is to sow a few seeds in mid-spring under cloches to provide plants for seeding in late summer. Then sow a few more successively into summer to give a regular supply of fresh young foliage. Pick leaves and

Right: *A versatile ingredient for many dishes.*
Left: *Dill (*Anethum graveolens*).*

flower heads fresh, and seedheads before seeds fully ripen, and then allow them to dry naturally. Take care not to allow the plants to become very dry between waterings or to suffer any other checks to growth.

Dill Basics

Problems: None.

Recommended Varieties: Normal species only is available.

Ornamental Appeal: Delicate, feathery, green foliage, umbels of small yellow flowers.

Site and Soil: Full sun, in light, free-draining but fertile soil. Will never succeed in cold or wet situations.

Hardiness: Fairly hardy, tolerating about −5°C (23°F) but almost invariably grown as an annual.

Size: Will attain about 60cm–1m × 50cm (24in– 3ft × 20in) in one summer.

Dill Uses

Culinary Chopped leaves can be used to flavour cooked fish, cream cheese, soups and other dishes. Seed is used with fish, soups and some confections. Flower heads are added to pickled cucumbers and other pickled vegetables. Seeds and flower heads used to make dill vinegar.

Non-Culinary Various, principally dill water for digestion.

Angelica archangelica

Garden Angelica

The range of flavours offered by the family Apiaceae, often called umbellifers, never ceases to amaze. What greater contrast could there be, for instance, between the assertive aniseed of fennel and the gentle sweetness of angelica? Like many other umbellifer, it is a white-flowered plant of damp places but it falls into the more robust group with less finely divided leaves and with stout stems.

Above: Angelica archangelica.
Right: *Crystallized angelica.*

Cultivation and Care

Although an herbaceous perennial, it is best grown as a biennial, sowing seed in growing positions in spring. Cut down to soil level in autumn then mulch. Mulch again in spring and give a light dressing of balanced general fertilizer. Harvest leaves in early summer, then stems for crystallizing and, finally, seedheads in late summer.

Garden Angelica Basics

Problems: None.

Recommended Varieties: Normal species only is available.

Ornamental Appeal: No special distinction to separate it from other umbellifers; umbels of small, greenish-white flowers held above its large, light green leaves.

Site and Soil: Partial shade in moist, preferably organic soils.

Hardiness: Very hardy, tolerating −20°C (−4°F) or below.

Size: Will attain about 2m × 75cm (7ft × 30in) by second year.

Garden Angelica Uses

Culinary Stems are crystallized for decorating confectionery, leaves are used in compotes of rhubarb and other fruits to reduce tartness, seeds to flavour gin and other drinks.

Non-Culinary Several minor medicinal uses, including an infusion as a treatment for flatulence; also roots and other parts are used as a source of pleasant sweet aromas (the development of these two uses is to be considered purely coincidental).

Anthriscus cerefolium

Chervil

Chervil is an annual, domestic relative of that most common of European wild umbellifers, the white-flowered cow parsley, *Anthriscus sylvestris*. The foliage is very similar, although chervil is a much shorter-growing plant. While cow parsley has no garden virtues, chervil is a valuable species with one of the more elusive herbal flavours, described variously as aniseed, myrrh and parsley, although

it is not quite like any of these. It has long been appreciated by French chefs and reference to *cerfeuil* will often be found on French menus.

Cultivation and Care

Grow as a hardy annual, sowing in growing positions under cloches in mid-spring, thinning plants to about 20cm (8in) spacing. May be allowed to self-seed if space allows.

Chervil Basics
Problems: None.

Recommended Varieties: Normal species only is available.

Left: *Crush chervil in a mortar or with your hand before use.*
Opposite: *Garden chervil (Anthriscus cerefolium).*

Ornamental Appeal: Pretty, very finely divided leaves and white flower heads with a rather neat overall habit.

Site and Soil: Light shade, in light, moist, but definitely free-draining soils.

Hardiness: Moderately hardy, tolerating about −10°C (14°F).

Size: Attains 30–45 × 30cm (12–18 × 12in) within a year.

Chervil Uses

Culinary Chopped leaves are used in salads and with a wide range of cooked dishes such as chicken and many fish that do not themselves have strong flavours.

Non-Culinary Several minor medicinal uses, usually raw leaves for digestive well-being.

Apium graveolens

Wild Celery, Smallage

The cultivated varieties of celery are now among the less commonly grown kitchen garden vegetables, largely because the trenched types require rich organic soil and considerable care and attention, while the self-blanching types have little to commend them. But in a large herb garden, space should be found for the wild plant which has a long and interesting history stretching back to classical times when it was used, along with olives, parsley and other plants, to make wreathes for the victors in the ancient Greek games.

Cultivation and Care

Grow as a hardy annual or a biennial, sowing in growing positions in mid-spring and then thinning plants to about 35–45cm (14–18in) spacing. It may flower and seed in the first year but if not, mulch in the autumn, give a little balanced fertilizer in spring and wait until the second summer to harvest the seeds.

Wild Celery Basics

Problems: Fungal leaf spot.

Recommended Varieties: Normal species only for herbal interest; cultivated variants if you wish to grow them as vegetables.

Ornamental Appeal: Rather pretty, small, slightly divided leaves and umbels of greenish-white flowers.

Site and Soil: Light shade, in rich, moist, but definitely free-draining soils.

Hardiness: Very hardy, tolerating −20°C (−4°F).

Size: Attains 80cm–1m × 30cm (32in–3ft × 12in) usually by the second year.

Above: *Wild celery (*Apium graveolens*) is an unusual salad ingredient.*
Left: *Growing wild celery.*

Wild Celery Uses

Culinary Seed is used to make celery salt; chopped leaves in salads and with a number of cooked dishes, especially fish.

Non-Culinary Used historically for medicinal purposes, and now known to have a very high vitamin content.

Armoracia rusticana

Horseradish

There aren't many herbs that can turn on their owners in quite the way horseradish can. It will even surpass mint in its invasiveness and ineradicability, and really must be kept well confined from the outset. It should, ideally, be planted in a pit lined with bricks or stone slabs, but even these should be mortared together or it will force its way through the joints. But do not let this put you off growing this most valuable culinary plant. There is certainly no comparison between freshly prepared horseradish sauce and the bland, shop-bought mixture so often used.

Cultivation and Care

It is an herbaceous perennial but the best way to grow horseradish for root production and to keep its vigour within bounds is as an annual. Set aside an area of soil about 75cm × 75cm (30 × 30in), ideally confined by stone slabs sunk vertically, and plant two or three plants in spring. Dig up in autumn and either use the roots immediately to make sauce or store them frozen until required. Inevitably, pieces of root will be left in the ground to renew growth in the following year. Give a top-dressing of compost mulch and also balanced general fertilizer in early spring.

Horseradish Basics

Problems: Leaf-attacking insects although none are that serious; also mildew and club-root (although this is uncommon).

Recommended Varieties: Normal species is widely available but a prettier variant, 'Variegata', with white leaf blotches is sometimes seen and its culinary value seems to be no different.

Ornamental Appeal: Almost none, apart from the variegated form. Large, strap-like fresh green leaves, small white flowers are produced unpredictably in the late summer on a tall spike.

Left: Armoracia rusticana.
Below: *Grated horseradish.*

Site and Soil: Almost any; although horseradish grows best in full sun and good soil, experienced gardeners will know that it is perfectly capable of growing anywhere.

Hardiness: Very hardy, tolerating −20°C (−4°F) or below.

Size: Will attain about 75cm– 1m × 30cm (30in– 3ft × 12in) within a year if grown, as suggested, as an annual plant.

Horseradish Uses

Culinary Roots, grated or, even better, minced to make sauce for use with meat and smoked or oily fish. An excellent variation is made by mixing in chopped, cooked beetroot.

Non-Culinary Several minor medicinal uses, including a treatment for coughs and other throat complaints.

Arnica montana

Arnica

This herbaceous perennial is one of those plants that few people ever see, as it has become something of a rarity, and even fewer can name it; it tends to be dismissed as 'another' yellow-flowered daisy. Yet it is pretty enough in its natural habitat of dry montane grasslands and in the herb garden where it has been grown for many centuries for various medicinal uses.

Above: *Arnica flower* (Arnica montana).
Right: *Drying arnica flowers.*

Cultivation and Care

Mulch lightly in the spring and autumn and give a light dressing of balanced general fertilizer in spring. Cut down top growth in autumn. Propagate by division in autumn or spring; can also be seed sown in spring in a humus-enriched, soil-based compost in a cold-frame.

Arnica Basics

Problems: Mildew, but generally only after flowering.

Recommended Varieties: Normal species only is available.

Ornamental Appeal: Downy, hairy leaves in an attractive rosette from which the single, rather lax, yellow daisy flowers arise in summer.

Site and Soil: Full sun, in acidic, free-draining but a fairly rich soil.

Hardiness: Very hardy, tolerating −20°C (−4°F) or below.

Size: Will attain about 50–75 × 30cm (20–30 × 12in) after about four years.

Arnica Uses

Culinary None; it should not be taken internally.

Non-Culinary Several minor medicinal uses, especially to produce an external treatment for sprain and strain relief; also for a herbal tobacco produced from the dried roots and foliage.

Artemisia spp.

Artemisia

Artemisias are among the unsung heroes of the herb garden. They are never really spectacular and, with the best will in the world, most can't truly be described as attractive although there are some striking forms with silver leaves. Yet among these herbaceous perennials are some of the oldest and most traditional of medicinal herbs as

well as, in tarragon, one of the most individual and valuable of culinary plants. The Greeks knew the value of artemisias and the genus is named after no less a personage than the sister of the classical king Mausolus, whom she buried in a magnificent tomb (hence, mausoleum). But despite her no-doubt very busy life, Artemisia still found time to grow and study herbs; a lesson for us all.

Right: *A bunch of fresh tarragon.*
Left: *French Tarragon (*Artemisia dracunculus*).*

Cultivation and Care

Mulch lightly in spring and autumn and give a balanced general fertilizer in spring. Cut back to a few centimetres above the crown in autumn. Propagate by semi-ripe cuttings in summer, rooted in a soil-based compost in a cold-frame.

Artemisia Basics

Problems: None.

Recommended Varieties: The best variety, the authentic tarragon, is *Artemisia dracunculus* with narrowly elongated, glossy leaves and a subtle, slightly aniseed-like flavour. The more narrowly leaved, so-called Russian tarragon *A. dracunculoides* is a most inferior plant and no substitute for the former.

A. arborescens (old woman) is more shrubby than most species with tufted, silvery and soft foliage. *A. abrotanum* (southernwood, old man or lad's love) has finely divided leaves with a scent of lemon. *A. absinthium* (wormwood) is an extremely bitter-tasting plant with finely divided leaves; the most attractive form is the very silvery 'Lambrook Silver' widely grown as an ornamental.

A. caucasia (also called *A. lantata* or *A. pedemontana*) has very soft, silky

73

and fairly finely divided leaves. *A. lactiflora* (white mugwort) has much less finely divided, toothed, light green leaves. *A. ludoviciana* var. *latiloba* (western mugwort, white sage) has willow-like leaves with a silvery sheen, most marked in the ornamental varieties 'Silver Queen' and 'Valerie Finnis'. *A. pontica* (Roman wormwood) has pretty, very feathery foliage and a strong, rather spicy smell.

Ornamental Appeal: Finely divided and aromatic foliage, very silvery in the best selected forms.

Site and Soil: Full sun, in light, free-draining, preferably slightly alkaline soil.

Hardiness: Most are moderately hardy, tolerating −15°C (5°F) or below, provided mulch protection is given to the crowns in winter.

Above: *Dried tarragon.*
Left: *Southernwood (*Artemisia abrotanum*).*

Size: Varies with species; most will attain 90cm– 1m × 30– 45cm (34in– 3ft × 12– 18in) within three years; but *A. caucasia* is a low-growing, ground-cover species while *A. lactifolia* tends to be taller than most and can reach 2m (7ft).

Artemisia Uses

Culinary Tarragon leaves have numerous uses, especially when combined with chicken but also to make tarragon vinegar and herb butter, tartar sauce, hollandaise sauce and other purposes. Other *Artemisia* species are of little culinary value although some have been used to flavour alcoholic drinks, most notably absinthe.

Non-Culinary Tarragon has several minor medicinal uses and was once employed as a treatment against scurvy (the plant is now known to be rich in vitamin C). The leaves of other *Artemisia* species are used as a source of insect repellents in homes and gardens; formerly used as a treatment for internal human parasites, they also had various minor medicinal uses as general antiseptics.

Atriplex hortensis

Orache

The large extent of the spinach family, Chenopodiaceae, isn't appreciated by most people nearly as much as that of the cabbage family, Brassicaceae, and orache – a hardy annual – is one of its least familiar members even though it has been cultivated in herb gardens for centuries and was once a very important medicinal plant. There are native species of orache, all more or less acceptable as substitutes for spinach but this, the herbal form, was originally an Asian plant.

Cultivation and Care

Sow seed in pots and then transplant at spacings of 60 × 60cm (24 × 24in), alternating coloured-leaf forms if they are available.

Orache Basics

Problems: Mildew, leaf-attacking insects.

Recommended Varieties: A golden-leaved form and a reddish-purple-leaved variant called *rubra* are sometimes available and look attractive interplanted alongside the normal green-leaved plant.

Ornamental Appeal: Large, more or less triangular leaves, unspectacular in the plain green-leaved form but striking in the coloured variants. Orache is a large plant, however,

Left: Atriplex *(orache).*
Right: Atriplex hortensis rubra *(red orache).*

and its much-branched habit means that it should be planted with due consideration for its impact. Flowers are tiny and carried in unassuming, dock-like heads.

Site and Soil: Full sun, in free-draining but fairly rich soil.

Hardiness: Very hardy, tolerating −20°C (−4°F) or below.

Size: Will attain up to 2m × 75cm (7ft × 30in) within a year.

Orache Uses

Culinary Strictly speaking, none as a herb although the coloured forms make a very pretty addition to salads. It is popular in France where it is used as a salad vegetable and basis for soups.

Non-Culinary Once important medicinally for its general healing properties and very widely used as the basis of a treatment for sore throats.

Bellis perennis

Daisy

Dandelions, clover, speedwell – most people want to control these lawn weeds; yet very rare is the person who wants his or her lawn freed from *Bellis perennis*, the little white and golden lawn daisy. Perhaps it is because it's pretty, perhaps because it doesn't spread with quite the aggressiveness of most weeds, or perhaps it's simply that we all have memories of childhood games. None of this explains its presence in a herb garden, however, and yet it really is worth growing for its charming flowers alone, which look wonderful in salads.

Cultivation and Care

Very little needed. May be grown as an annual but best as a small perennial group, given a little balanced fertilizer in spring and divided every few years. When it's grown in this manner, you will be surprised how many gardeners fail to recognize it as the same plant that grows on their lawns.

Daisy Basics

Problems: None.

Recommended Varieties: The normal species is the one for herb garden use; the selected colour forms and doubles just don't have the same appeal.

Above: *Spring salad with edible flowers.*
Left: *Daisy flowers (*Bellis perennis*).*

Ornamental Appeal: Familiar single daisy flowers with white, pink-tipped rays and golden discs; a very neat, rosette habit.

Site and Soil: Almost any but best in full sun or very light shade, and least successful on very light, free-draining soils.

Hardiness: Very hardy, tolerating −20°C (−4°F) or below.

Size: Will attain about 15 × 15cm (6 × 6in) after about two or three years.

Daisy Uses

Culinary Flowers and leaves can be used in salads (but be sure not to pick them from a lawn that has been treated with weedkiller at any time).

Non-Culinary Several minor medicinal uses, the leaves in particular are used to make an external treatment for bruises.

Borago officinalis

Borage

Borage provides some of the most pleasant herbal experiences, either when admired growing in the garden or when used as a garnish in cold drinks. This annual is also a source of frustration, however, for it does self-seed with abandon and seedlings must be pulled out ruthlessly. For many gardeners, it has the most attractive flowers in the entire family Boraginaceae and the closer you examine them, the lovelier they are. It is one of the essentials of any herb garden and, understandably, has been admired for centuries and has a considerable associated folklore.

Cultivation and Care

Sow, in the first instance, in growing positions and then allow to self-sow each year and simply remove any unwanted seedlings.

Borage Basics

Problems: None.

Recommended Varieties: The normal species is the one to grow although there is a white form, 'Alba', which seems a rather pointless variant. There is also a rather uncommon form with variegated foliage.

Right: *Borage ice cubes.*
Left: *Borage flower (*Borago officinalis*).*

Ornamental Appeal: Beautiful, small, single, pointed flowers of electric-blue.

Site and Soil: Prefers either full sun or very light shade and light, free-draining but not at all impoverished soil.

Hardiness: Very hardy, tolerating −20°C (−4°F) or below.

Size: Will attain about 60– 75 × 30cm (24– 30 × 12in) within a year or so.

Borage Uses

Culinary Flowers can be used for decoration in salads and, most appealingly, in cold drinks. Add single flowers to the compartments of ice cube trays; when the ice subsequently melts in the glass, the flowers will float out. The young leaves may also be used in salads and cooked like spinach.

Non-Culinary Several minor medicinal uses, including, again like many other herbs, a treatment for external inflammation.

Brassica spp.

Mustards

For most gardeners, brassicas are vegetables, and the genus *Brassica* certainly embraces some of the most important crops in the kitchen garden: cabbage, cauliflower, Brussels sprout, kale, to name a few. But there are also the brassicas for which the seeds, rather than the leaves or flowers, are more important and these, the mustards, should find a place in the herb garden if you have room for them; they are, however, large plants. But try home-grown mustard and you will be loathe to buy anything in a bottle again.

Cultivation and Care

Grow as a hardy annual, sowing seed into growing positions and thin to about 15cm (6in). May self-seed but as they will hybridize freely, it is best to sow fresh using bought or specially saved seed each spring.

Mustard Basics

Problems: Leaf-attacking insects, mildew and club root.

Recommended Varieties: The naming of many cultivated brassicas is both contentious and very confusing, all the more so since plants hybridize very readily and because, especially with the vegetable species, the cultivated forms bear little resemblance to any wild plants. There are, however, three important mustard species named, after their seed colours, as white, black and brown and these are generally called *B. hirta*, *B. nigra* and *B. juncea*. *B. nigra* is the true 'mustard and cress' mustard that imparts the tangy flavour.

Above: *Black mustard seeds.*
Left: *Mustard flower (*Brassica hirta*).*

Ornamental Appeal: Bright yellow, typical Brassica flowers in summer.

Site and Soil: Full sun or very light shade and light, free-draining but fertile soil.

Hardiness: Very hardy, tolerating −20°C (−4°F) or below.

Size: Varies considerably with species: white mustard will attain 45–75 × 25cm (18–30 × 10in); black mustard and brown mustard 1–2m × 75cm (3–7ft × 30in).

Mustard Uses

Culinary Seeds are used to make mustard sauce; use black or brown seeds and grind them into a little cold water. Use white seeds as a preservative in pickles. Young leaves and flowers can also be used to add spiciness to salads, sandwiches and many other savoury dishes.

Non-Culinary Various medicinal uses, most notably to produce a healing warm bath for the feet and also used as an emetic to induce vomiting.

Calamintha grandiflora

Calamint

Labiates and umbellifers undoubtedly vie for the most important role in the herb garden. This plant is a rather typical labiate in its upright, angled stem, its opposite pairs of leaves and its lipped flowers, but it is very commonly seen as a component of a herbaceous perennial border. There is no apparent reason for this, apart from the fact that the flowers are appealingly deep pink or purple instead of the usual labiate insipid mauve. This calamint is from southern Europe and Asia and does have the merit of a pleasing mint-like perfume. For years it has been put to various medicinal uses.

Cultivation and Care

Mulch in spring and autumn and give some balanced general fertilizer in autumn. Cut down all above-ground growth in autumn.

Calamint Basics

Problems: None.

Recommended Varieties: The normal species is most usually seen but there is a variegated-leaved form, 'Variegata'.

Ornamental Appeal: Rather little; erect spikes of typically labiate form with pink or purple flowers in summer.

Site and Soil: Light to moderate shade as it is naturally a woodland plant, in free-draining, moderately rich, preferably alkaline soil.

Hardiness: Very hardy, tolerating −20°C (−4°F) or below.

Size: Will attain about 45 × 30cm (18 × 12in) after two or three years.

Left and right: *Calamint (*Calamintha grandiflora*).*

Calamint Uses

Culinary None.

Non-Culinary The dried leaves are used to make a somewhat peppermint-flavoured tea, said to be good, like so many other herbs, for the digestion.

Calendula officinalis

Pot Marigold

A favourite annual herb for many, pot marigold is often thought of as *the* traditional marigold – the vulgar-flowered African and French newcomers just don't hold a candle to it. It has a simplicity and honesty that allows it to flaunt the gaudiest of orange shades and yet not seem crude. It has been a garden plant for so long that its origins are lost in time but nothing else contrasts so happily with the fresh greens of summer salads as these hot, vibrant flame and amber tones, be they in the garden or in the salad bowl.

Cultivation and Care

Sow seed in growing positions in mid-spring and thin plants to a spacing of about 12cm (5in). Dead head regularly. It's best when it can be allowed to self-seed but this is not successful on all sites and re-sowing each year may be necessary.

Pot Marigold Basics

Problems: Mildew, but generally only after flowering is over.

Recommended Varieties: There are many selected forms and mixtures, the modern types including reds and yellows as well as the more familiar clear orange. 'Orange King' is a good

choice for those who prefer the taller, pure orange forms.

Ornamental Appeal: Striking double or semi-double, bright orange flowers on stiff stems with fresh green leaves.

Site and Soil: Full sun or very light shade, tolerates most soils but best in not-too-rich, free-draining sites.

Hardiness: Very hardy, tolerating −20°C (−4°F) or below.

Size: Varies with variety but the better, older forms will attain about 45 × 30cm (18 × 12in) within the year.

Above: *Salad with dill, nasturtium and marigolds.*
Left: *Pot marigold (Calendula officinalis).*

Pot Marigold Uses

Culinary Flowers, either whole or as individual florets, are used in salads and also cooked dishes including cheese recipes, soups and omelettes. Leaves are also used in salads.

Non-Culinary Various extracts, as well as the raw leaves, have been used to make healing preparations for skin bruises and wounds.

Cardamine pratensis
Lady's Smock, Cuckoo Flower

With softly coloured single- and double-flowered species, this herbaceous perennial is one of the more unexpected and most dainty plants for the herb garden. It is ideal for damp conditions and will help to attract a number of butterfly species. According to folklore, this charming plant is sacred to fairies and should not, therefore, be taken indoors.

Cultivation and Care

Little needed once the plant is established but it will benefit from a light dressing of any balanced general fertilizer in the spring.

Lady's Smock Basics

Problems: Mildew, occasionally club root.

Recommended Varieties: The normal, wild species and the double 'Flore Pleno' are both commonly seen in nurseries and are equally valuable as herbs.

Ornamental Appeal: Small, very pale pink flowers and divided leaves in a basal rosette.

Site and Soil: Light to moderate shade, in damp, fairly nutrient-rich soil.

Hardiness: Very hardy, tolerating −20°C (−4°F) or below.

Size: In good growing conditions, it will attain 45– 60 × 15cm (18– 24 × 6in) after two years.

Above: *Cuckoo flower (*Cardamine pratensis).
Left: *Cuckoo flower in a meadow.*

Lady's Smock Uses

Culinary Rather tangy leaves can be added to salads, or are good simply to nibble in the garden.

Non-Culinary Various minor medicinal uses, particularly as the basis of a cough remedy and as a source of vitamin C.

Carthamus tinctorius

Safflower, False Saffron

Plants prefixed with the name 'false' are either closely related to the real thing or are put to similar uses. In this case it is the latter, for while 'genuine' saffron is produced from a species of *Crocus*, it is very costly and this Asian annual daisy yields a useful substitute. Both in the wild or in the herb garden, it is a striking ornamental and worth having, even if you don't want home-grown pretend saffron.

Cultivation and Care

Grow as a moderately hardy annual, raising seedlings under glass in spring, and plant out when they are large enough to handle.

Safflower Basics

Problems: Mildew.

Recommended Varieties: Various colour selections are sometimes available but the normal species is the one to choose for herbal use; and it is more attractive too.

Right: *Safflower (*Carthamus tinctorius*).*
Opposite: *Vibrant* Carthamus *petals*.

Ornamental Appeal: Robust, thistle-like flowers with reddish-orange florets on stems with quite large, bristly leaves.

Site and Soil: Full sun, in light, fairly rich but definitely free-draining soil.

Hardiness: Hardy, tolerating about −15°C (5°F) but not important as it is grown as an annual.

Size: Will attain about 1m × 30cm (3ft × 12in) within a year.

Safflower Uses

Culinary Florets can be used as a substitute for saffron as a food colouring agent; commercially, cooking oil is extracted from the seeds of this plant.

Non-Culinary Several medicinal uses including seed extracts that have been used to lower blood pressure and flowers prepared as the basis of laxatives.

Carum carvi

Caraway

Caraway is a popular herb today; its seeds are recommended in a great many recipes and are readily available at food stores. It is, however, an ancient herb plant and can be one of the trickier umbellifers to grow well in colder climates as it is among those plants that are always reminding you that their natural home is somewhere a little warmer. In appearance, this biennial is very much

like any other, relatively low-growing, white-flowered member of its family, and it is closely related to parsley.

Cultivation and Care

Grow as a moderately hardy annual but sow seeds in growing positions in spring in rows 15– 20cm (6– 8in) apart and thin plants to 15cm (6in) spacing. Like most umbellifers, the tap root is easily damaged if transplanted. Do not cut down after first year but harvest the seeds when they are ripe at the end of the second summer.

Left: *Caraway in flower (*Carum carvi*).*
Right: *Caraway seeds, with their characteristic ribbed appearance.*

Caraway Basics

Problems: None.

Recommended Varieties: Normal species only is available.

Ornamental Appeal: Rather minimal, with feathery foliage and some small white flowers in umbels.

Site and Soil: Full sun, in light, fairly rich but free-draining soil.

Hardiness: Hardy, tolerating about −15°C (5°F).

Size: Will attain about 60 × 20cm (24 × 8in) within two years.

Caraway Uses

Culinary Numerous uses for the seeds; as a flavouring in bread and confectionery, in soups and particularly important in Indian and other Asian cooking; also scattered over fattier types of meat and poultry. Roots may be boiled as a vegetable but are a bit wiry and uninteresting, and leaves may be used in salads.

Non-Culinary Minor medicinal uses, principally to aid digestion but also, just as with parsley, chewing caraway seeds or leaves is pretty effective at killing the smell of garlic on the breath provided it is done fairly promptly after the garlic has been eaten.

Cedronella canariensis

Balm of Gilead

Balm of Gilead is one of those names that you imagine only occur within the pages of the Bible and, just as with myrrh and frankincense, it comes as something of a surprise to discover that such things really exist. The true, biblical balm of Gilead is a species of aromatic shrub and this herbaceous perennial is one of a handful of other species that have acquired the name through having a somewhat similar fragrance. Its romantic name and associations might lead you to expect something rather special but it is a bit of a let-down being yet another of those rather anonymous labiates, worthy of inclusion in a collection for its perfume, but best not given pride of place.

Cultivation and Care

Best grown as a half-hardy annual, sowing seed in warmth in early spring and then growing the plant in a container that can be stood outside once the danger of frost has passed. It should then be discarded because, even as a perennial, it is short-lived.

Balm of Gilead Basics

Problems: None.

Recommended Varieties: Normal species only is available.

Left: *Balm of Gilead pink flower head.*
Below: *Balm of Gilead (*Cedronella canariensis*).*

Ornamental Appeal: Very slight, with small pinkish flowers in terminal heads, and elongated, dull green leaves.

Site and Soil: Full sun, in light, fairly rich but free-draining soil; or in a good soil-based potting compost in a container.

Hardiness: Barely to fairly hardy, tolerating about −5°C (23°F).

Size: Will attain about 1m × 30cm (3ft × 12in) within a season, if raised initially in warmth.

Balm of Gilead Uses

Culinary None.

Non-Culinary Leaves are a source of heavy, sweet perfume.

Chamaemelum nobile

Chamomile

Chamomile lawns have been grown for centuries, including at, among other places, Buckingham Palace. But whether or not you aspire to such sophisticated gardening, there's no denying that one of the flowering chamomiles should be in every herb collection. They look good, they smell good and, if all herbalists are to be believed, they do you good, too.

Cultivation and Care

Little needed once this herbaceous perennial is established but best divided every three or four years as it tends to turn brown in the centre and die back. Trim off flower heads when fresh if required for potpourri or as they fade if not. Give a light dressing of any balanced general fertilizer in spring.

Chamomile Basics

Problems: None.

Recommended Varieties: The lawn chamomile is 'Treneague', a non-flowering variant of the herb garden species, although the double-flowered form 'Flore Pleno' is lovely and could be chosen for herbal use instead.

Left: *Double Chamomile (Chamaemelum nobile 'Flore Pleno').* **Right:** *Chamomile tea is said to have a calming effect.*

The rather similar-looking German chamomile, *Matricaria recutita*, with similar uses, is an annual easily raised from seed. Another daisy, the pretty golden-flowered *Anthemis tinctoria*, is known as dyer's chamomile.

Ornamental Appeal: Very soft, feathery foliage and low-growing habit above which the small, individual daisy flowers are borne.

Site and Soil: Full sun, in quite light, fairly rich but free-draining soil.

Hardiness: Very hardy, tolerating about −20°C (−4°F) but browned in cold winters.

Size: Will attain about 25 × 30cm (10 × 12in) in three years.

Chamomile Uses

Culinary None.

Non-Culinary Flowers are used to produce chamomile tea, said to have all manner of beneficial properties including the prevention of bad dreams. An extract from the flowers is used for conditioning hair.

Chenopodium bonus-henricus

Good King Henry

There are numerous suggestions for how this herbaceous perennial obtained its name and which King Henry was being honoured but the consensus appears to be that its old name was mercury and that, in Germany, dog's mercury (*Mercurialis perennis*), which is poisonous, is called bad Henry; so this one is called 'good' to distinguish it. This is a species that has been cultivated for centuries and it both looks and tastes rather like spinach. It's one of those plants that straddles the boundary between herbs and vegetables but since it is now a relatively uncommon plant, it can be called a herb.

Above: *Good King Henry (*Chenopodium bonus-henricus*).*

Cultivation and Care

Give a balanced fertilizer in spring, keep well watered during the summer, cut down most of the top growth and mulch in autumn. Divide every two years.

Good King Henry Basics

Problems: Leaf-attacking insects, mildew, fungal leaf spots.

Recommended Varieties: Normal species only is available.

Ornamental Appeal: About the same as spinach, which isn't very often grown for the beauty of its appearance.

Site and Soil: Full sun or very light shade, in rich, well fertilized and free-draining soil.

Hardiness: Very hardy, tolerating −20°C (−4°F).

Size: Will attain about 60 × 30cm (24 × 12in) within about three years.

Above: *Good King Henry flower head.*

Good King Henry Uses

Culinary Leaves are cooked and eaten like spinach, also young leaves fresh in salads and young flower heads like broccoli. Some suggest that young shoots make a tolerable substitute for asparagus.

Non-Culinary None of any great significance.

Cichorium intybus

Chicory

Salad chicory with its characteristic, electric-blue daisy flowers is indeed a glorious thing. A versatile plant, the various species span a number of uses both culinary and non-culinary. It is a native of Europe and has become widely naturalized in North America and Australia.

Cultivation and Care

The following advice is intended for the cultivation of chicory for other than mainly vegetable purposes. The plants are best grown as hardy annuals and should only be kept as perennials if they are required for ornamental use only. Sow seed in growing positions in spring, ideally with cloche protection to give as long a growing season as possible. Mulch once plants are large enough, give a balanced general fertilizer and then lift roots either for forcing or roasting when the top growth dies down in autumn.

Chicory Basics

Problems: Downy mildew, leaf-attacking insects, stem rot.

Left: *Chicory (*Cichorium intybus*).*
Right: *Chicory root.*

Recommended Varieties: It's important to select the correct variety for each purpose. If your interest is mainly ornamental, choose the normal species although if you want variation, the white- and pink-flowered forms *album* and *roseum* are available. If you want to grow your own coffee substitute, you can make do with the 'Witloof' types or the normal species, or if you can find it, the selected variety 'Brunswick'. The rather bitter, lettuce-like vegetable, radicchio, is also a form of chicory.

Ornamental Appeal: Rather gaunt, twiggy appearance when mature but compensated for by the superb blue flowers.

Site and Soil: Full sun, in rich, well fertilized and free-draining soil, preferably alkaline.

Hardiness: Hardy, tolerating about −15°C (5°F).

Size: Will attain 1.2– 1.5m × 45cm (4– 5ft × 18in) by the late autumn after an early start from seed.

Chicory Uses

Culinary Flowers used in salads, roots as a vegetable or dried, roasted and ground as a coffee substitute. Roots may also be dug in autumn, kept in compost in the dark and will produce chicons, the cylindrical, blanched leafy shoots used as a slightly bitter but very tasty winter salad.

Non-Culinary Various minor medicinal preparations from leaves and roots; the roots are a laxative.

Claytonia perfoliata

Winter Purslane, Miner's Lettuce

The name 'miner's lettuce' implies that this is a poor relation of something better, though many find this much tastier as a winter salad plant than most of the lettuce that is sold at that time of the year. Its drawback is its smallness, for you need a lot of purslane to make a plateful. It isn't a relative of lettuce, or even of spinach but a member of the family that includes the ornamental alpine genus, *Lewisia*, and also an equivalent summer crop, *Portulaca oleracea* (see page 210), the summer purslane. You might still find it in some seed catalogues under its old name of *Montia*.

Cultivation and Care

Grow as a hardy annual, sowing sequentially in growing positions from spring to late summer, providing cloche protection at start of season and then through the winter. Sow in rows approximately 20cm (8in) apart and then thin the plants to 15cm (6in) within rows. Pick leaves on the cut-and-come-again principle; pull or cut away leaves as they are needed and more will grow to give further crops.

Right: *Miner's lettuce (*Claytonia perfoliata*).*

Right: *Miner's lettuce leaves rinsed and ready for cooking.*

Winter Purslane Basics

Problems: None.

Recommended Varieties: Normal species only is available

Ornamental Appeal: Not great as it looks like a weed and, to many gardeners, it probably is. Small, rounded, pale green leaves and tiny white flowers in summer on rather tall stalks.

Site and Soil: Full sun, in light, fairly rich but quite free-draining soil.

Hardiness: Very hardy, tolerating −20°C (−4°F) but may be damaged in cold winters.

Size: Will attain 25– 30 × 15– 20cm (10– 12 × 6– 8in).

Winter Purslane Uses

Culinary Leaves are used as salad, especially in winter, or cooked and served as spinach.

Non-Culinary None.

Coriandrum sativum

Coriander, Cilantro

Coriander is another of those herbs that has soared in familiarity and popularity with the increased interest, in recent years, in oriental cooking. It is yet another of those white-flowered umbellifers and, like so many of them, is strongly aromatic although it is an aroma that some find a bit unpleasant; something that can be understood more when one discovers that its name might be derived from the Greek word for bedbug.

Cultivation and Care

Grow as a hardy annual, sowing in growing positions in spring and then again in summer for overwintering under cloches. Sow in rows 20cm (8in) apart and thin plants to 15– 20cm (6– 8in) within rows. Pick the leaves when they are young and fresh and

harvest the seeds before they are shed naturally in the autumn.

Coriander Basics

Problems: None.

Recommended Varieties: Normal species only is available.

Ornamental Appeal: Very slight for the gardener, although the contrast between the fine, feathery upper leaves and the broader, more parsley-like lower ones is rather pleasing on the eye.

Site and Soil: Full sun, in light, moderately rich, free-draining soil.

Hardiness: Fairly hardy, tolerating about −5°C (23°F) but may be damaged in cold winters.

Size: Will attain 30–50 × 25–30cm (12–20 × 10–12in).

Left: *Coriander leaves are pleasing to both eye and tongue.*
Above: *Coriander seeds.*

Coriander Uses

Culinary Seeds are used in curries, oriental dishes, soups, sauces, pickles, chutneys and in confectionery and pastries. Leaves are also used in soups, curries and other dishes. Stems and roots can be cooked and incorporated in dishes or served alone as a vegetable.

Non-Culinary Several minor medicinal uses; sometimes used simply to disguise the taste of less pleasant medicines since it has such a strong distinctive flavour.

Dianthus spp.

Pinks, Carnation

The entire notion of eating flowers is pretty alien to some gardeners. Gradually, however, their visual and edible appeal has become more widely appreciated; but this hasn't spread as far as the genus *Dianthus*, which is still used to provide button-holes at weddings. But the petals of many varieties make interesting additions to a number of dishes. In classical times it was considered the flower of the heavens or the gods.

Cultivation and Care

Grow as short-lived herbaceous perennials, giving a light dressing of balanced general fertilizer in spring but don't mulch as this tends to cause stem base rotting. Cut down dead flower heads as they fade. Take cuttings in the late summer and root in a free-draining, soil-based compost in a cold-frame. Discard the plants after about three years when they become straggly and unkempt.

Right: Dianthus.
Opposite: Dianthus *flowers make a pretty addition to any table, on a plate or in a vase.*

Pinks Basics

Problems: Virus, leaf spots, leaf-attacking insects, thrips.

Recommended Varieties: All the hardy outdoor *Dianthus* species may be used, including the clove-scented pinks, the maiden pinks, border carnations and the *Dianthus* Allwoodii pinks.

Ornamental Appeal: Very pretty flowers in a wide range of colours, the most attractive being the old clove-scented pinks with their frilled petals and lacy patterning.

Site and Soil: Full sun, in light, moderately rich, free-draining and preferably alkaline soil.

Hardiness: Hardy, tolerating about −15°C (5°F) but may be damaged in extremely cold winters.

Size: Varies with type but will generally attain 30–60 × 30cm (12– 24 × 10– 12in) within three years although they don't really attain this full height as they have a flopping, sprawling habit.

Pinks Uses

Culinary Coloured parts of petals are used in salads, desserts, with omelettes, with meat dishes and other foods, according to scent and flavour. Also to flavour vinegar and sugar and as the flavouring of a syrup to serve with sweet dishes.

Non-Culinary A few minor medicinal uses.

Dictamnus albus

White Dittany, Gas Plant

This is just one of several 'burning bushes' and it isn't the biblical one. The name is used for plants that produce a volatile and inflammable vapour that can be ignited, something that may happen spontaneously in very hot climates. This one isn't even a bush but a herbaceous perennial, superficially a bit like a low-growing delphinium although it is a relative of rue (see page 224). It tends now to be grown as an ornamental border perennial but it does have a very long and varied history as a herbal plant, too.

Cultivation and Care

Mulch in autumn and spring, give a balanced general fertilizer in spring, cut down dead flower spikes in autumn; should not need staking. Divide every three or four years in autumn. May be propagated from seed but not all colour forms come true and are very slow to flower, so they are better increased by division.

Left: Dictamnus albus.
Right: *Medicinal tea made from burning bush leaves.*

White Dittany Basics

Problems: None.

Recommended Varieties: The normal species is widely available, as is *purpureus*, a variety with pink, red-veined flowers.

Ornamental Appeal: Rather pleasing, fragrant, fresh green leaves divided into numerous oval leaflets with spikes of flowers which, despite the name, offer a choice of either white, red, pink or purple.

Site and Soil: Full sun or light to moderate shade, in most soils provided they are fertile and not very heavy and wet.

Hardiness: Very hardy, tolerating −20°C (−4°F).

Size: Will attain 50– 75 × 30cm (20– 30 × 12in) within about three years.

White Dittany Uses

Culinary Leaves are used to produce a scented tea.

Non-Culinary Numerous medicinal uses, mainly as a pain-relieving treatment for conditions such as cramp, rheumatism and kidney stones.

Echium vulgare

Viper's Bugloss

The Boraginaceae is a most extraordinary family of plants, spanning forget-me-nots at one end and the almost tree-sized echiums of the Canary Islands and Africa at the other, with a great many rather bristly-leaved things in between. This biennial echium, native to most of Europe and common in North America, is far from tree-sized. It is unclear why it should be associated with vipers but it is one of many rather similar plants that have been found or claimed to have herbal value.

Cultivation and Care

Sow seeds into growing position in summer, do not stake or cut down in autumn, give a light dressing of balanced general fertilizer in spring but do not mulch. Best when allowed to self-seed.

Right: *Viper's bugloss seeds.*
Left: *Viper's bugloss (*Echium vulgare*).*

Viper's Bugloss Basics
Problems: None.

Recommended Varieties: Normal species only is available.

Ornamental Appeal: Tolerably attractive pink and blue flowers on a rather coarse, branched spike and elongated, oval, bristly leaves.

Site and Soil: Full sun, in light, free-draining, preferably alkaline soils.

Hardiness: Very hardy, tolerating −20°C (−4°F).

Size: Will attain 75–90 × 30cm (30–34 × 12in) by the second summer of growth.

Viper's Bugloss Uses
Culinary Flowers used in salads.

Non-Culinary Several minor medicinal uses for leaf extracts, including the relief of pain and fever; also seed extracts, apparently, to bring cheer.

Equisetum arvense

Field Horsetail

It's only with the greatest hesitation that this plant is included because, in many other contexts, it is considered the most ineradicable of weeds. You should consider planting it if you really are determined to have a truly comprehensive herb collection, and then only with great circumspection. If nothing else, there is always a special fascination in a spore-bearing plant that has existed in almost unaltered form for many millions of years.

Cultivation and Care
No attention needed, but if this herbaceous perennial is to be planted deliberately, this should be in a deep, lined pit as described for horseradish (see page 68).

Field Horsetail Basics
Problems: None.

Recommended Varieties: The normal species only is available.

Ornamental Appeal: There is a curious attraction in the Christmas-tree-like overall appearance and a fascination in the rather asparagus-like spore-bearing stems.

Above: *Horsetail foliage.*
Left: *The spore-bearing stems of horsetail (*Equisetum arvense*).*

Site and Soil: Full sun to light shade, will grow almost anywhere but always most vigorous and invasive on any light, free-draining soils.

Hardiness: Very hardy, tolerating −20°C (−4°F).

Size: Will attain 45–60 × 30cm (18–24 × 12in) within two years but spreads very rapidly by far-reaching rhizomes.

Field Horsetail Uses

Culinary A rather curious-tasting tea can be made from the stems; otherwise none.

Non-Culinary Used to make a wound-healing poultice for external relief.

Eruca vesicaria

Salad Rocket, Arugula

Rocket is a familiar sight on many menus and indeed a familiar ingredient in many kitchens. In fact, we can pay handsomely for what, for years, has been a waste-ground weed. This is simply a consequence of it having escaped from cottage gardens where it has been grown for centuries for its herbal value. Indeed, so widespread is it now that its true geographical origin is unknown. It is an unremarkable looking crucifer, but has a delicious slightly tangy flavour.

Cultivation and Care

Best to sow this annual in growing positions in succession from early spring to mid-summer, making first sowings under cloches and placing cloches on in the autumn to give protection in winter. Space rows 12cm (5in) apart and thin to 30cm (12in) within rows. Keep well watered especially in dry periods to reduce the chance of bolting.

Salad Rocket Basics

Problems: Flea beetles, mildew, club root.

Left: *Rocket (*Eruca vesicaria sativa*) in a kitchen garden.*
Right: *Fresh, washed baby rocket.*

Recommended Varieties: The normal species is widely available, although the cultivated form is sometimes given a separate name as *Eruca sativa*.

Ornamental Appeal: Minimal – rather like a small cabbage that has run to seed, or an under-fed oil seed rape.

Site and Soil: Full sun or light shade, in rich, well manured soil, preferably slightly alkaline although any good vegetable soil will be suitable.

Hardiness: Very hardy, tolerating −20°C (−4°F).

Size: Will attain 60– 90 × 30cm (24– 34 × 12in) but only reaches full height in flower and is best picked before it reaches this.

Salad Rocket Uses

Culinary Leaves are used to add spiciness to otherwise bland salads; they can also be cooked like spinach. The white flowers, too, are edible but unremarkable.

Non-Culinary Few medicinal uses but once very important when seeds were used most extensively as the basis of a cough preparation.

Eryngium maritimum

Sea Holly, Seaside Eryngo

Most gardeners now appreciate the value of the sea hollies (all 230 species of them) as border ornamentals, but persuading people to eat them might be another matter. Only *Eryngium maritimum* is worth eating, but it does need the correct conditions if it is to be successful. This herbaceous perennial certainly looks like nothing else that is likely to be growing in your kitchen garden and the most unexpected thing about it is that it is an umbellifer.

Cultivation and Care

Mulch in spring and autumn and give a very light dressing of balanced general fertilizer in spring. Leave dead flower heads on over winter and cut old growth back in spring. Propagate by

division in spring or from seed, sown in early spring under cloches, with the plants then grown as biennials.

Sea Holly Basics

Problems: Mildew.

Recommended Varieties: The normal species only for herbal use.

Ornamental Appeal: Interesting, pale bluish-green spiky, holly-like leaves with tiny flowers in bluish heads.

Site and Soil: Full sun, in light, free-draining, relatively nutrient poor soil; remember its natural habitat is on sand dunes.

Hardiness: Hardy to very hardy, tolerating −15°C (5°F) but liable to damage by harsh, cold winter winds.

Size: Will attain 60– 75 × 30– 45cm (24– 30 × 12– 18in) within three or four years.

*Left: Sea holly (*Eryngium maritimum*).*
Right: The blue stems and leaves of this sea holly are specific to a Cretan variant. It seems to thrive in association with the more common green-leaved variety.

Sea Holly Uses

Culinary Shoots with young unopened flowers and with leaves stripped off are boiled or steamed like asparagus. Young leaves may be similarly cooked.

Non-Culinary Several medicinal uses, mainly with root extracts which have some healing and soothing properties.

Eupatorium purpureum

Trumpet Weed

A native of North America, where it is also called Joe Pye weed or gravel root – presumably referring to its value as treatment for bladder stones – this is an eyecatching addition to any ornamental border or herb garden. An herbaceous perennial, it does double duty by attracting butterflies and other wildlife.

Cultivation and Care

Mulch in spring and autumn and apply a balanced general fertilizer in spring. Cut back dead top growth in autumn. It may need staking on windy sites. Propagate by division in the spring or the autumn.

Right: Eupatorium purpureum.
Opposite: *Dried trumpet weed root.*

Trumpet Weed Basics

Problems: None.

Recommended Varieties: There are several selected colour forms for ornamental use but, as a herb garden plant, the normal species is ideal.

Ornamental Appeal: Striking, tall stems with appealing, elongated, fresh green leaves and dark reddish heads of tiny daisy-like flowers with delicate feathery heads.

Site and Soil: Full sun to moderate shade, in fairly rich, moist, preferably alkaline soil.

Hardiness: Very hardy, tolerating −20°C (−4°F).

Size: Will attain 2.5– 3 × 1m (8– 10 × 3ft) within three or four years.

Trumpet Weed Uses

Culinary None.

Non-Culinary Several medicinal uses, including making from the root an extract with which to treat bladder stones.

Euphrasia officinalis
Eyebright

This plant is a real challenge; but then it's not every day that you are advised to grow a parasite in your garden. To be precise, the eyebright is a semi-parasite for it has normal green leaves for photosynthesis but is also partly parasitic on grass roots, and it is this habit that makes its cultivation a challenge. When you can grow it, however, this annual is a pretty thing and was once widely used in country areas for its herbal properties, hence its common name.

Cultivation and Care
There are two ways of establishing eyebright and once done, it should self-seed. The first is to find a farmer with the plant growing on his or her grassland and ask to remove a small square of turf that can be transferred to your garden. The other option is to buy seeds, either eyebright only or as a wild flower meadow seed mixture known to include eyebright, and sow these on an area of rather poor, prepared soil, which has been cleared of clay, big stones and weeds.

Left: *Eyebright (*Euphrasia officinalis*).*
Right: *Eyebright flowering stems.*

Eyebright Basics

Problems: None.

Recommended Varieties: Normal species only is available.

Ornamental Appeal: Rather pretty, with small, white and pinkish flowers in creeping, branched rather hairy stems.

Site and Soil: Full sun, in light, free-draining alkaline soil.

Hardiness: Very hardy, tolerating −20°C (−4°F).

Size: Will attain about 20 × 10cm (8 × 4in) within a year but once established, individual plants are hard to distinguish within the overall mat of growth.

Eyebright Uses

Culinary None.

Non-Culinary Important medicinal uses were for sore throats, allergies such as hay-fever and also as an eye treatment, although no medicament should be applied to eyes without qualified advice.

121

Filipendula ulmaria

Meadowsweet, Queen of the Meadow

Meadowsweet is one of the plants most evocative of summer days, redolent with the hum of insects and a slight heat haze above

the water meadow. The herbal value of meadowsweet was discovered a long time ago, and it must surely always have been a plant that people noticed. What is always a surprise, nonetheless, is to know that this herbaceous perennial is a member of the rose family but perhaps the leaves are the biggest giveaway – rather like those of a large potentilla.

Cultivation and Care
Mulch in spring and autumn, give a balanced general fertilizer in spring. Cut down top growth in autumn.

Left: Filipendula ulmaria.
Right: *Dried and fresh flowers of meadowsweet.*

Divide every three or four years in autumn. Propagate by division or seed sown in spring in soil-based, humus-enriched compost in a cold-frame.

Meadowsweet Basics
Problems: None.

Recommended Varieties: For herb garden use, choose the normal species; the coloured-leaved and double-flowered forms are more appropriate for the herbaceous border.

Ornamental Appeal: Very pretty, feathery, cream and very fragrant (hence the name, meadowsweet) flower heads on very tall stems.

Site and Soil: Full sun to light or almost moderate shade, in moist, rich, fertile, preferably alkaline soil.

Hardiness: Very hardy, tolerating −20°C (−4°F).

Size: Will attain about 1m × 45cm (3ft × 18in) within three or four years.

Meadowsweet Uses
Culinary Flowers are used as flavouring in wines and home-made beer and in various desserts and confections.

Non-Culinary Long known to have pain-relieving properties; aspirin was eventually isolated from the flower buds. It was also one of the most popular strewing herbs, used for spreading on the floor in the days before carpets.

Foeniculum vulgare

Fennel

Fennel is one of the indispensable herbs, as much for its appearance as for its herbal value. It is a big plant, a very big plant if you consider the small amount that is needed in cooking, as its flavour is very strong. The beautiful yellow heads are such a welcome change from the run-of-the-mill, white umbellifers and the foliage is some of the loveliest in the entire family.

Cultivation and Care

Mulch in spring and autumn, give a balanced general fertilizer in spring. Cut down top growth in late autumn and divide every three or four years in autumn. Propagate by division or by seed sown in spring in soil-based compost in a cold frame. An herbaceous perennial, fennel self-seeds readily and many gardeners are loath to plant it for this reason but it is not really a problem provided the seedlings are pulled out promptly before the tough tap-root begins to take grip.

Right: *Fennel (*Foeniculum vulgare*).*
Opposite: *Fennel seeds.*

Fennel Basics

Problems: None.

Recommended Varieties: Always remember that the vegetable fennel or finnocchio, with swollen stem bases is a separate variety, *dulce*. For herbal use, choose the normal species or the bronze-leaved variant, now usually called variety 'Purpureum'.

Ornamental Appeal: Beautiful feathery foliage in fresh, bright green or rich bronze with heads of rich yellow flowers on tall stems.

Site and Soil: Full sun or light shade, in fairly rich, free-draining good loam.

Hardiness: Very hardy, tolerating −20°C (−4°F).

Size: Will attain about 1.5–2m × 60cm (5–7ft × 24in) within three or four years.

Fennel Uses

Culinary Seed and chopped leaves are used for aniseed flavour in fish dishes, salads, sauces and soups. Tender young stems can be chopped and also used in salads. As it is the easiest to grow of the aniseed-flavoured umbellifers, it may be used as a substitute for others.

Non-Culinary Various minor medicinal uses, including an infusion from the seeds used as a treatment for constipation.

Fragaria vesca

Wild Strawberry

You may have all sorts of reasons for growing any particular plant in your herb garden but the wild strawberry will probably fit none of them. For a start it is a fruit and, you might think, merely a smaller, weedier version of the domestic varieties. In reality, it's a fascinating plant that played a part in the ancestry of some of the cultivated forms, exceeds almost all of them in the flavour of its tiny fruit and also has herbal uses for its leaves.

Cultivation and Care

This herbaceous perennial may be raised from seed but is best obtained as plants. If planted in a bed, space 30cm (12in) each way but it is more attractively and appropriately planted as the edging to a herb garden. Mulch lightly in spring and autumn, give a light dressing of a balanced fertilizer in spring and trim off foliage to a few centimetres above the crown after fruiting is finished, at the end of the summer. It may be necessary to throw netting over the fruiting plants as protection from birds although they tend to be much more interested in the large-fruited varieties.

Left: *Wild strawberry (*Fragaria vesca*).*

Right: *For many, a bowl of wild strawberries epitomizes summer.*

Wild Strawberry Basics

Problems: Slugs, mildew.

Recommended Varieties: Normal species only is the one to choose; the closest among cultivated varieties are the so-called Alpine strawberry types such as 'Baron Solemacher'.

Ornamental Appeal: Small, white and yellow flowers in spring followed by small red fruit. Characteristic and familiar three-lobed, fresh green leaves.

Site and Soil: Best in light shade, in light, free-draining, preferably alkaline soil.

Hardiness: Very hardy, tolerating −20°C (−4°F).

Size: Will attain about 25 × 25cm (10 × 10in) and spreads by runners; these may be trimmed off to keep plants more compact.

Wild Strawberry Uses

Culinary Fruit is used as cultivated strawberries but leaves also used with cooked meat to improve flavour and as an ingredient of herbal teas.

Non-Culinary Leaf tea for intestinal and urinary problems.

Galega officinalis

Goat's Rue, Professor-Weed

This is another one of those species with an inexplicable name; it isn't related to the common rue as it is a member of the pea family, Fabaceae, and the association with goats seems obscure unless it has something to do with the old use of the juice in cheese-making to clot milk. Or it might just be because of its peculiar smell. It is a big plant that won't fit into many herb gardens and is an example of those species that are perhaps better kept for a herb border where it will look rather pretty if unstartling.

Cultivation and Care

Mulch in autumn and spring and give a dressing of balanced general fertilizer in spring. Cut down top growth in autumn. Propagate this herbaceous perennial by division or by seed sown in spring in a soil-based compost in a cold-frame.

Goat's Rue Basics

Problems: Mildew may be a problem if summers are hot.

Right: *Goat's rue tea.*
Left: *Goat's rue*
*(*Galega officinalis*).*

Recommended Varieties: Normal species only is the one to choose although a white-flowered form, 'Alba', is also available.

Ornamental Appeal: Terminal clusters of mauve, pea-like flowers with typical, much-divided, pea-like leaves.

Site and Soil: Full sun, in rich, fertile, preferably moist organic soil.

Hardiness: Very hardy, tolerating −20°C (−4°F).

Size: Will attain about 1m × 60cm (3ft × 24in) after three years.

Goat's Rue Uses

Culinary Juice squeezed fresh from stems will clot milk.

Non-Culinary Infusions made from the dried flowers were used apparently to stimulate milk flow in nursing mothers, while seed extracts have also been used to treat diabetes, but such practices should never be carried out without medical supervision.

Galium spp.

Woodruff, Bedstraw

Galium is a lovely genus of small, generally pretty but unspectacular and inoffensive plants, although it does include that slightly troublesome annual weed, goosegrass. There are two members well worth including in the herb garden, the sweet woodruff and the lady's bedstraw, both with the whorls of tiny leaves so typical of the genus and heads of the most minute flowers that *en masse* have a delicate, feathery appearance. The appropriately named sweet woodruff was a highly valued plant in earlier centuries, widely used as a strewing herb and in herb pillows.

Above: *Woodruff (*Galium odoratum*).*
Right: *Glass of woodruff tea.*

Cultivation and Care

Mulch lightly in autumn and spring and give a dressing of any balanced general fertilizer in spring. Cut down top growth in autumn. Propagate these herbaceous perennials by division or by seed sown fresh in late summer in soil-based compost and left to overwinter outdoors.

Woodruff Basics

Problems: None.

Recommended Varieties: The two normal species *Galium odoratum* and *G. verum* are the only ones available.

Ornamental Appeal: Pretty, small leaves in whorls with terminal masses of tiny white or yellow flowers.

Site and Soil: Full sun, in rich, fertile, moist but well drained soil.

Hardiness: Very hardy, tolerating −20°C (−4°F).

Size: *G. odoratum* will attain about 30–45 × 25cm (12–18 × 10in) after two or three years; *G. verum* is a more sprawling plant but can attain double this.

Woodruff Uses

***G. odoratum* Sweet Woodruff**

Culinary Long known for the refreshing drink made from the dried leaves, known in Germany as the May Bowl Punch. It is generally prepared by adding sweet German or Alsace wine to the dried leaves with sugar and lemon juice and then a small quantity of brandy.

Non-Culinary Several minor medicinal uses.

***G. verum* Lady's Bedstraw**

Culinary Leaves used in cheese making to curdle milk while the flowers give it a yellow colours.

Non-Culinary None.

Genista tinctoria

Dyer's Greenweed

Greenweed is a pretty unimaginative name for a plant, although the prefix 'dyer's' indicates fairly unambiguously its most important use. Yes, this shrubby perennial was once a very important source of a yellow dye and although it has no culinary herbal use and only one dubious medicinal one, it is included here regardless of the decline in its use for dyeing, because it is one of those plants that is no longer as familiar as it once was.

Cultivation and Care

Mulch in autumn and spring and give a dressing of balanced rose fertilizer in early spring; prune very lightly after flowering to remove old and overcrowded growth.

Dyer's Greenweed Basics

Problems: None.

Recommended Varieties:
The normal species is widely available but there are selected ornamental forms including the double-flowered 'Flore

Right: *Dyer's greenweed stems with (left to right) leaves, flowers and fruit.*
Left: *Dyer's greenweed (Genista tinctoria, 'Royal Gold').*

Pleno' and 'Royal Gold' with strikingly golden flowers; both have a more trailing habit than the normal species.

Ornamental Appeal: Narrowly elongated, rather dull green leaves with spikes of yellow, pea-like flowers in summer followed by pea-like pods.

Site and Soil: Full sun, in light, free-draining, moderately rich and preferably alkaline soil.

Hardiness: Very hardy, tolerating −20°C (−4°F).

Size: Normal species will attain about 1.5m × 75cm (5ft × 30in) but some of the selected forms are much lower growing than this.

Dyer's Greenweed Uses

Culinary None.

Non-Culinary Once used medicinally but now thought too toxic to be used safely.

133

Glycyrrhiza glabra

Licorice

Few plants are so inextricably associated with childhood and schooldays as licorice. And yet how many of those who sucked licorice candy or even chewed the raw licorice root that was once available (and perhaps still is), could describe the plant from which it originates. An herbaceous perennial, it is, in truth, a large, rather coarse although moderately attractive Mediterranean member of the pea family.

Cultivation and Care

Mulch in autumn and spring and give a dressing of balanced general fertilizer in the early spring; lift and divide in autumn or, in milder areas, in spring and harvest roots as needed.

Licorice Basics

Problems: None.

Recommended Varieties: Normal species only usually available although there are selected culinary forms.

Ornamental Appeal: Rather coarse plant with large, divided leaves and narrowly elongated, generally rather sticky leaflets; upright stems of mauve or darker violet flowers.

Site and Soil: Full sun, in rich, preferably organic but free-draining soil.

Hardiness: Moderately hardy, tolerating about −15°C (5°F).

Size: Will attain about 1.5m × 75cm (5ft × 30in) within about three years.

Above: *Licorice root.*
Left: *Licorice (*Glycyrrhiza glabra*) foliage.*

Licorice Uses

Culinary Roots contain an extremely sweet-tasting substance called glycyrrhizin used to flavour confectionery and drinks.

Non-Culinary Root extract is used to produce a laxative and also a preparation for coughs and throat ailments.

Helianthus annuus
Sunflower

There can't be many garden plants that are as instantly familiar and generally well loved as the sunflower. It's a North American species that was cultivated there since ancient times and is now grown all over the world for its spectacular growth rate and striking appearance, almost unmatched by any other half-hardy annual.

Cultivation and Care

Raise as a half-hardy annual; it is best to sow directly into the growing position which should be prepared in advance by digging in plenty of well-rotted manure and compost, similar to summer squash or pumpkins. Sow about two weeks before the likelihood of the last frost. To obtain sunflowers of really impressive proportions, it is essential to water regularly, apply liquid fertilizer at least once a week and stake the plants, replacing the stake as the stem elongates.

Sunflower Basics

Problems: Insect pests will attack the leaves but rarely cause much harm; mildew may also occur but not generally until after flowering has ceased.

Recommended Varieties: There are many selected varieties of sunflower, some of them dwarf. If it is to be

grown as a representative of its species, however, you should choose a big variety and, in order for you to obtain a crop of seeds, it should be single- rather than double-flowered. 'Russian Giant' is as good a variety as you will find.

Ornamental Appeal: Impressive and almost too well known to justify description: very tall leafy stems topped by massive, golden-yellow flowers of characteristic daisy form.

Site and Soil: Full sun with shelter from winds, in rich, preferably organic but free-draining soil.

Hardiness: Barely hardy, liking no less than −5°C (23°F).

Size: This depends on how assiduously you water and feed; 'Russian Giant' can reach 5.5m (17ft); but when choosing a position to sow, remember that the spread is also about 1m (3ft).

Sunflower Uses

Culinary The seed kernels are delicious, either on their own or in salads, and either raw or after roasting. The oil is widely used in cooking and the seeds may also be sprouted and eaten in salads. The unopened flowers may be cooked and eaten in the same manner as globe artichokes (a strange state of affairs as sunflowers are closely related to the Jerusalem artichoke).

Non-Culinary Seeds and oil have been used to make preparations for the relief of gastric and kidney problems.

Left: *Radiant sunflowers (*Helianthus annuus*).*
Above: *Sunflower seeds.*

Helichrysum italicum

Curry Plant

This southern European native is not the answer to making your own curry; it only smells as if it is. The main garden purpose of the curry plant is to look pretty, and its striking leaves and flowers achieve

this admirably. It is also sometimes suggested as a plant for edging knot gardens, but, in truth, not even the dwarf form of this shrubby/herbaceous perennial is really neat enough for this purpose.

Cultivation and Care

Mulch in autumn and spring and give a dressing of balanced general or rose fertilizer in early spring; trim lightly in the spring to remove winter-damaged shoots and maintain a neat shape. Propagate by semi-ripe cuttings rooted in a gritty, soil-based compost in a cold-frame in summer.

Left: *Curry plant (*Helichrysum italicum*).*

Right: *Curry plant shoots make a useful flavouring.*

Curry Plant Basics

Problems: None.

Recommended Varieties: The normal species is widely available; the dwarf form appears to have no generally accepted name.

Ornamental Appeal: It has silver, needle-like leaves with heads of tiny, yellow button flowers.

Site and Soil: Full sun, in light, free-draining, moderately rich soil.

Hardiness: Moderately hardy, tolerating around −10°C (14°F) and may in consequence die back to soil level in cold winters.

Size: Will attain about 45– 55 × 30cm (18– 22 × 12in) in two or three years.

Curry Plant Uses

Culinary Sprigs will add a mild curry flavour to dishes but it is not strong enough to substitute for the real thing.

Non-Culinary None.

Hesperis matronalis

Sweet Rocket

The name sweet rocket tends to be used only when this plant is grown as a herb. Wild flower gardeners and observers probably know it better as dame's violet. It is very recognizably a member of the cabbage family, Brassicaceae, and looks as if it ought to have yellow, not lilac-coloured flowers. It has been grown for centuries, partly for its herbal value and partly for its flowers, at their fragrant best late in the day.

Cultivation and Care

Best grown as a biennial, with seeds sown in pots of soil-based compost in early summer for planting out in early autumn to flower in the following year. Will then self-seed and throw out new shoots from the base after flowering to become semi-perennial.

Right: Hesperis matronalis *'Alba'*.
Left: Hesperis matronalis.

Sweet Rocket Basics

Problems: Mildew, caterpillars, flea beetles.

Recommended Varieties: The normal species is widely available and probably best for herb garden use although there are also white and double-flowered forms.

Ornamental Appeal: Simple, characteristically brassicaceous flowers in shades of lilac or white, on slender stems with less characteristically brassicaceous, sword-shaped leaves.

Site and Soil: Full sun or very light shade, in fairly rich, preferably organic, moist soil.

Hardiness: Very hardy, tolerating −20°C (−4°F).

Size: Will attain 75cm–1m × 30cm (30in– 3ft × 12in) by the second year.

Sweet Rocket Uses

Culinary Leaves and flowers may be added to salads although leaves, especially, should be used with care as they have a very strong flavour except when very young.

Non-Culinary Minor, largely obsolete medicinal uses but was used to treat scurvy.

Humulus lupulus

Hop

The traditional methods of picking and pruning hops entail balancing on wooden stilts 4m (13ft) high in the middle of a hop garden, as the commercial plantations are known. This illustrates that although a herbaceous perennial, a hop in full flight is mighty and is a climber that should be planted with caution.

Cultivation and Care

Best grown on a screen or other free-standing support rather than against a wall. Mulch in autumn and spring and give a balanced general fertilizer in spring. No pruning needed but cut back all top growth to about 30cm (12in) above soil level in late autumn and then back to soil level in spring. Propagate by semi-ripe cuttings in late summer in a sand and peat mixture in a propagator with some bottom heat.

Hop Basics

Problems: None.

Recommended Varieties: As there is probably no difference in the herbal properties, the best plant to grow is the golden-leaved variety, 'Aureus', but whether you choose this or the normal species, it is important to buy named female plants to be sure of obtaining the attractive cone-like female flowers.

Ornamental Appeal: Large, coarsely toothed, rather vine-like leaves and unexpectedly dainty, cone-like female flowers.

Site and Soil: Full sun, with shelter from cold winds, in rich, moisture-retentive loam.

Size: Once established, will attain 7 × 2m (22 × 7ft) within a growing season.

Above: *It is thought that 'beer' (a brew using hops) originated in Germany.*
Left: *Hop (*Humulus lupulus*).*

Hop Uses

Culinary It is the dried female flower cones that are used to flavour beer but the young leaves and stems may be blanched and eaten as a vegetable or in soup.

Non-Culinary The flowers are very mildly sedative and for this reason have not only been used to make tea-like infusions but are also included, dried and put in herbal pillows.

Hydrastis canadensis

Yellow Root, Golden Seal

This North American herbaceous perennial is one of the lesser known members of the buttercup family but if you are expecting beautiful, golden-yellow buttercup flowers, you will be in for a disappointment. It has a curious appeal, nonetheless, in its little greenish-white blooms that lack petals and have instead petaloid sepals. It should certainly be included in any comprehensive herb collection for it has in the past had important medicinal uses.

Cultivation and Care

Mulch in autumn and spring and give a dressing of balanced general fertilizer in the early spring. Cut back above-ground growth in late autumn. Propagate by division in autumn or from seed sown in the spring in a soil-based compost in a cold-frame.

Yellow Root Basics

Problems: None.

Recommended Varieties: Normal species only is available.

Ornamental Appeal: Rather limited; small, petal-less flowers in late summer and tiny, inedible, dark red fruits on hairy stems with somewhat coarse, lobed leaves.

Site and Soil: Best in partial shade, in moist, but not waterlogged, rich, organic soil.

Hardiness: Very hardy, tolerating −20°C (−4°F).

Size: Will attain about 40 × 25 cm (16 × 10in) after two or three years.

Yellow Root Uses

Culinary None.

Non-Culinary Small amounts of the yellowish dye obtained from the roots seem to contain an antiseptic ingredient, as they have been used successfully to treat various ulcerous lesions.

Left: *Golden seal (*Hydrastis canadensis*).*
Above: *The roots of golden seal are used in herbal medicine.*

Hypericum perforatum
St John's Wort

There are a great many species of *Hypericum*, most of them called
St John's Wort, and a fair proportion of them only of moderate value
as garden plants. On ornamental grounds, this very variable species
would join their number but it has a number of herbal uses that
justify its inclusion here. The genus as a whole is characterized by
tiny dots on the leaves that can be seen when they are held up to the
light. These dots are glands yielding the oil that confers the various
herbal properties.

Above: *St John's Wort (*Hypericum perforatum*).
Right: *Essential oil of* Hypericum perforatum.

Cultivation and Care

Mulch in the autumn and spring and give a dressing of balanced general or rose fertilizer in the early spring. Above-ground growth may be left on, in shrub fashion, but is best cut back hard in spring every second year. The best method of propagation for this shrubby/herbaceous perennial is by the removal of naturally rooted runners in autumn or spring.

St John's Wort Basics

Problems: None.

Recommended Varieties: Normal species only is available.

Ornamental Appeal: Rather limited; masses of small, star-like yellow flowers with small, elongated, pale green leaves on a rather woody, sprawling plant.

Site and Soil: Full sun or light shade; tolerates most soils as long as they are not very heavy and waterlogged.

Hardiness: Very hardy, tolerating −20°C (−4°F).

Size: Will attain 75cm– 1m × 40– 50cm (30in– 3ft × 16– 20in) after two or three years.

St John's Wort Uses

Culinary Young leaves may be added to salads to give a slightly tangy flavour.

Non-Culinary Extracts from the flowers have been used to produce a treatment for bruises and similar lesions.

Hyssopus officinalis

Hyssop

Hyssop is one of the best known of garden herbs. A shrubby/ herbaceous perennial, it is, like so many others, a member of the family Lamiaceae but not only does it have a wide range of herbal uses, it is also rather pretty in any of its variably and extensively coloured forms. It is a plant best reserved for the middle part of the herb garden, because although it is certainly good enough to be noticed, it is not quite up to front-of-the-bed high standard.

Cultivation and Care

Mulch lightly in autumn and spring and give a dressing of balanced general or rose fertilizer in early spring. Above-ground growth is best cut back hard in the spring. Propagate

by the semi-ripe cuttings method in
the early summer using a soil-based
compost in a cold-frame.

Hyssop Basics

Problems: None.

Recommended Varieties: The normal
blue-flowered species is widely
available but selected forms are
offered as *albus* (white), *roseus* (pink),
purpurescens (purple) as well as large-
flowered variants.

Ornamental Appeal: Spikes of small,
labiate flowers in a range of colours on
neat, rather bushy plants with massed
and narrowly elongated leaves.

Site and Soil: Full sun, in light, free-
draining, preferably alkaline soil.

Hardiness: Very hardy, tolerating
−20°C (−4°F).

Size: Will attain 75 × 30cm (30 × 12in)
within each season after being
cut back.

Above: *Hyssop herbal tea.*
Left: Hyssopus officinalis.

Hyssop Uses

Culinary Young leaves and flowers
add a spicy flavour to salads while
leaves may be cooked with a wide
range of meat dishes as well as
being used in fruit compotes
and pies.

Non-Culinary Leaf infusions have
been used to treat a number of
internal complaints while wound-
healing preparations have also
been produced from the infusion
of leaves.

Inula helenium

Elecampane

This striking member of the Asteraceae family is one of those herbs that could be a perfectly worthy member of the ornamental herbaceous border. Its leaves are a little large in proportion to its flowers, perhaps, but they are of a lush, fresh green colour and serve well enough their purpose of setting-off the blooms. This herbaceous perennial is now widely naturalized in Europe although it came originally from northern Asia. *Helenium* is said to derive from the story that Helen of Troy was collecting the plant when she was carried off by Paris.

Left: *Elecampane (*Inula helenium*).*
Right: *Herbal remedies can be made from elecampane root.*

Cultivation and Care

Mulch in spring and autumn and give any balanced general fertilizer in autumn. Cut down above-ground growth in autumn. It is best staked in summer as it can flop rather untidily. Propagate by division in autumn.

Elecampane Basics

Problems: Mildew.

Recommended Varieties: Normal species only is available.

Ornamental Appeal: Large, fresh green, if slightly coarse leaves and small, rather short-rayed, golden-yellow daisy flowers in summer.

Site and Soil: Full sun, in rich, fairly moist but not waterlogged, loamy soil.

Hardiness: Very hardy, tolerating −20°C (−4°F).

Size: Will attain about 1– 2.5m × 50cm (3– 8ft × 20in) within three years, being much larger and much more lush in good growing conditions.

Elecampane Uses

Culinary The root may be cooked as a vegetable but it has a sharp, bitter taste no matter how long it is boiled for. A crystallized root extract is eaten as a confection. It has also been used to add flavour to a number of alcoholic drinks, of which absinthe is the best known.

Non-Culinary Root extract is used medicinally as an expectorant and cough relief.

Iris germanica var. Florentina

Orris Root

Iris is a huge and striking genus with a great many fine ornamental species. Surprisingly, however, it only encompasses one with herbal properties, the rather remarkable plant familiarly called *Iris florentina*, although now, more accurately, *I. germanica var. Florentina* for it is reckoned to be a variety derived from *I. germanica*. It is, therefore, a bearded iris, although smaller than the true species and much grown commercially, as its name suggests, in the neighbourhood of Florence. This herbaceous perennial is a notable plant in other regards too, generally being considered one of the irises that inspired the famous design of the fleur de lys of heraldry.

Left: *Orris root (*Iris germanica var. Florentina*).*
Right: *Roots from* Iris germanica var. Florentina.

Cultivation and Care

In general, bearded irises are best not mulched as this can encourage rotting of the surface rhizomes but they should be given a light dressing of a balanced general fertilizer or bone meal in the spring. Cut back flower stems as flowers fade and cut back foliage by about half in autumn. Does not need staking. Propagate by division of clumps after flowering. Reject the old, central area and shallowly replant the fresh young rhizomes.

Orris Root Basics

Problems: Slugs and snails.

Recommended Varieties: Normal variety only is available.

Ornamental Appeal: Typical, sword-like *Iris* leaves and very pale lavender or white flowers with yellow markings in early summer.

Site and Soil: Full sun, in rich, but free-draining, preferably slightly alkaline soil.

Hardiness: Very hardy, tolerating −20°C (−4°F).

Size: Will attain about 75cm–1m × 30cm (30in–3ft × 12in) within three years.

Orris Root Uses

Culinary None.

Non-Culinary The rhizome extract has been used medicinally as a very powerful purgative and also for other minor purposes although its greatest fame arises from its use to prepare orris, a sweetly scented product used in perfumery and other cosmetics.

Lamium spp.

Dead-nettles

Dead-nettles have nothing to do with stinging nettles and are quite harmless. There are several, very attractive species and varieties within the genus, well worth growing in the ornamental border. Some of these herbaceous perennials can legitimately find a home in the herb garden although, given the vast number of other herbs in the family Labiatae, this is really only to be expected.

Cultivation and Care

Mulch lightly in spring and autumn and give a balanced general fertilizer in spring. Cut down straggly, old flowering shoots towards the end of summer. Propagate by division in spring or autumn or by removal of naturally rooted runners.

Dead-nettles Basics

Problems: Mildew.

Recommended Varieties: Most of the herbal uses have been of the commonest species, *Lamium maculatum*, which exists in a wide number of varieties and among which the best are 'Beacon Silver' (richly silver foliage, pink flowers)

Right: *A cup of white dead-nettle tea.*
Left: *The white dead-nettle* Lamium album *is only superficially similar to the stinging nettle in its leaves.*

and 'White Nancy' (silver foliage and white flowers).

Ornamental Appeal: Small, toothed, heart-shaped leaves, low-growing habit and typical labiate flowers in summer.

Site and Soil: Full sun to moderate shade, in fairly rich, fairly free-draining soil but will flourish in most conditions.

Hardiness: Very hardy, tolerating −20°C (−4°F) or below.

Size: Will attain about 15 × 45cm (6 × 18in) within about three years.

Dead-nettles Uses

Culinary The young leaves can be used in salads, gently steamed as a vegetable or used in soups.

Non-Culinary A herbal tea may be made from dried leaves and a poultice of fresh leaves is said to have wound-healing properties.

Lavandula spp.

Lavender

Many thousands of gardeners grow lavenders in their gardens; and quite justifiably too for they are among the most evocative and (in most instances) beautifully scented of flowers that bloom in early summer. Lavenders are versatile too, being as valuable as low, ornamental hedging as they are massed in a border or used as individual specimens in pots or other ways. Everyone knows that they have long been used in perfumery but it may surprise many to realize that they have value as culinary herbs, too.

Cultivation and Care

Mulch in spring and autumn and give a balanced general or rose fertilizer in spring. Trim back with shears as the flowers fade, cutting a short way into the older wood to encourage a neat habit. Propagate this woody perennial by semi-ripe cuttings struck in a sandy, soil-based compost in a cold-frame in summer.

Lavender Basics

Problems: None.

Recommended Varieties: If you are to grow a lavender in your herb garden, it should be an attractive one but the herbal, and indeed perfume, value varies between the different types. The most familiar and most hardy lavenders are varieties of *Lavandula angustifolia* and include 'Alba', white flowers; 'Hidcote', rich purple flowers, neat habit, good perfume; 'Loddon Pink', taller habit, pink flowers; 'Munstead', similar to 'Hidcote' but with a rather more lax habit, slightly paler and earlier flowers; and the forms of *L.* x *intermedia*, which include 'Grappenhall', lavender-blue flowers, tall, rather lax habit; and 'Twickle Purple', neat compact habit, with purple flowers and soft, greyish leaves.

Above: *Lavender essential oil.*
Left: Lavandula angustifolia *'Heacham Blue'.*

Size: Varies with variety and pruning from about 45 × 30cm (18 × 12in) to 1m × 75cm (3ft × 30in) after three or four years.

Ornamental Appeal: Familiar spikes of flowers, by no means always lavender coloured and ranging from white to very dark purple. They are appealingly set off against the generally greyish-green, small leaves.

Site and Soil: Full sun, in fairly rich, but light and very free-draining soil. Lavenders will fail miserably in the cold and wet.

Hardiness: Very hardy, tolerating −20°C (−4°F or below) to fairly hardy, tolerating −5 to −10°C (23 to 14°F).

Lavender Uses

Culinary The flowers may be used in small quantities to flavour confectionery or even used in savoury dishes.

Non-Culinary Lavender tea, made from the flowers is said to be remarkably soothing and the oil has many applications in aromatherapy, in addition of course, to its use in perfumery.

Levisticum officinale

Lovage

Although many people have heard of lovage, few seem know what it looks like, and even fewer grow it. It is a very robust umbellifer (too robust for many gardens which accounts for its scarcity) with rather dirty-looking greenish-white flower heads and large, dark green and highly divided leaves. Its numerous herbal properties mean that this herbaceous perennial has been cultivated for centuries. If your herb garden is big enough, you should plant it.

Cultivation and Care

Mulch in the spring and autumn and give a balanced general fertilizer in spring. The plant may be treated much as any other herbaceous perennial and cut back to soil level in the

Left: *Lovage (Levisticum officinale).*
Right: *Dry lovage leaves.*

autumn although, if the stems are to be used, they are best cut young and, ideally, blanched by wrapping celery-blanching tubes around them. It is most readily propagated from seed; there will generally be self-sown seedlings available.

Lovage Basics

Problems: None.

Recommended Varieties: Normal species only is available.

Ornamental Appeal: The overall size and dark green leaves are the main attraction as the flowers are not very exciting.

Site and Soil: Full sun to light or moderate shade; will tolerate most soils, provided fairly rich and not waterlogged.

Hardiness: Very hardy, tolerating −20°C (−4°F) or below.

Size: Will attain 2m × 75cm (7ft × 30in) within two or three years.

Lovage Uses

Culinary The young leaves may be eaten in salads, added to cooked meat dishes, used to make a most pleasing soup or made into a refreshing tea. The seeds have traditionally been added to breads and pastries but may also be used to flavour savoury dishes. Roots and young stems may be cooked as a vegetable. Some say that, served with a sauce, the blanched young shoots are as good as asparagus.

Non-Culinary There are various minor medicinal uses, generally for relief of kidney complaints.

Lilium candidum

Madonna Lily

Not many bulbs can compete with lilies in the beauty and stateliness of their appearance so, on purely aesthetic grounds, it is pleasing that one at least finds a place in the herb garden. The Madonna lily is, in many ways, the archetypal cottage garden lily, unusual in being one of the handful of European species, one of the relatively few that fail in acidic soils, and probably unique in its preference for shallow planting.

Cultivation and Care

Always plant with the bulbs only just covered with soil. Mulch with leaf-mould in autumn and spring and give a dressing of bone meal in early spring. Cut off dead flower heads after the blooms fade and cut back the entire plant to soil level in autumn. Like all lilies, ideally grown in pots that can be moved away as the flowers fade. Propagate this bulbous perennial by division of bulb clumps in autumn or from seed, sown in warmth in any soil-based compost in early spring.

Madonna Lily Basics

Problems: *Botrytis*, lily beetle, slugs, virus; but generally rather less prone than many lilies to the disease problems, especially virus.

Recommended Varieties: The normal species is the one usually seen although there is a double-flowered variant, 'Plenum'.

Above: Lilium candidum *root.*
Left: *Madonna lily (*Lilium candidum*).*

Ornamental Appeal: Exquisite white, characteristically trumpet-shaped flowers in summer on rather spindly stems.

Site and Soil: Full sun, in light but rich and free-draining, preferably alkaline, soil.

Hardiness: Very hardy, tolerating −20°C (−4°F) or below.

Size: Will attain 1–1.5m × 25cm (3–5ft × 10in) within three years of planting a single bulb.

Madonna Lily Uses

Culinary The bulbs are cooked and eaten in parts of the eastern Mediterranean.

Non-Culinary An extract from the bulbs has long been used for softening hard skin, as in corns, and in ancient times, a vast number of other, generally fanciful attributes were claimed.

Linum usitatissimum

Flax

Familiar as the crop that colours country fields a glorious blue in the summer (a welcome change from the yellow of rape seed), flax is an ancient plant in cultivation and has both herbal interest and a simple beauty. It has had a surge in popularity recently because of the alleged health benefits conferred by flax seeds.

Above: *Flax (*Linum usitatissimum*).*
Right: *Flax seeds.*

Cultivation and Care

Grow as a hardy annual, either sowing seed *in situ* in spring or, if space is limited, raising a few plants in pots for planting out.

Flax Basics

Problems: None.

Recommended Varieties: The normal species is the best for the herb garden although various colour selections are offered as ornamental annuals.

Ornamental Appeal: Very flimsy-looking, tall, slender stems with usually small, single, blue flowers although white and red forms exist. The individual flowers are very short-lived but are renewed daily.

Site and Soil: Full sun, in light but moderately rich and free-draining soil.

Hardiness: Very hardy, tolerating −20°C (−4°F) or below.

Size: Will attain up to 1.2m × 15cm (4ft × 6in) (depending on various growing conditions) within the season.

Flax Uses

Culinary Both seeds and the fruits have traditionally been eaten and flax seeds, or linseeds, are now widely available as oil for salad dressings or simply as seeds to be sprinkled over salads and breakfast cereals.

Non-Culinary Seeds produce a laxative and are also used to make wound-healing poultices.

Lonicera caprifolium

Perfoliate Honeysuckle

Honeysuckle, in the generic sense, needs no introduction. Having both beautiful flowers and fragrance makes this perennial climber perfect. Perhaps too vigorous for small gardens but this is the species with the most effective herbal properties.

Cultivation and Care

Mulch in autumn and spring, preferably with leaf-mould, give a balanced rose fertilizer in spring. Cut back the oldest third of the shoots to soil level in spring and tidy up the overall structure. Propagated by semi-ripe cuttings in autumn in soil-based compost in a cold-frame.

Perfoliate Honeysuckle Basics

Problems: Aphids, mildew.

Recommended Varieties: The normal species is the one that is most suitable for the herb garden although there are one or two named variants with slightly more red-tinged flowers.

Right: Lonicera caprifolium *flowers.*
Opposite: *Honeysuckle has an unexpected use as a cut flower.*

Ornamental Appeal: Yellowish, pink-tinged flowers in summer, glaucous leaves, the uppermost united in pairs, and bright orange fruits.

Site and Soil: Best in light shade, and in rich, deep, organic loam.

Hardiness: Very hardy, tolerating −20°C (−4°F) or below.

Size: Will attain 4–5m (13–16ft) in height after three or four years and will flop outwards to a considerable distance.

Perfoliate Honeysuckle Uses

Culinary None.

Non-Culinary Apart from perfumery uses, the flowers and other parts have been used to produce products ranging from laxatives to cough treatments. As the tissues contain amounts of salicylic acid, the basis of aspirin, the efficacy of these is not unexpected, but means that the plant must be employed with caution.

Lupinus polyphyllus

Lupin

The appropriate lupin for the herb garden is this wild, North American species from which the garden varieties are derived. An herbaceous perennial, the flowers in the wild plant are generally blue although of course, a wide range of colours exists in the cultivated forms.

Above and right: *Lupin (*Lupinus polyphyllus*).*

Recommended Varieties: The normal species is the one for the herb garden; don't be seduced by anything else.

Ornamental Appeal: Familiar spikes of blue, lipped flowers in early summer; the spikes are never as tall in the wild forms as the cultivated species.

Site and Soil: Full sun or very light shade, in light but rich and free-draining soil.

Hardiness: Very hardy, tolerating −20°C (−4°F) or below.

Size: Will attain about 75cm– 1m × 50cm (30in– 3ft × 20in) after two or three years.

Cultivation and Care

Mulch in autumn and spring and give a dressing of balanced general fertilizer in spring. Cut back dead flower heads as soon as the flowers fade (unless seeds are required) and cut the entire plant down to soil level as soon as mildew disfigures it. Most easily propagated from seed.

Lupin Basics

Problems: Mildew and large lupin-specific aphids.

Lupin Uses

Culinary None; and should not be eaten as some parts, including the seeds, are toxic.

Non-Culinary A soothing skin preparation is made from seeds.

Malva moschata

Musk Mallow

There are several types of garden mallow, and several more types of plant with the epithet musk, but this particular one is unique because it combines the simply pleasing flower structure with the rich, heady musk fragrance. Several of the mallow species can be used to obtain the same herbal properties but it is this herbaceous perennial that is the prettiest and most manageable of them, and it has the added virtue of particularly attractive foliage.

Cultivation and Care

Mulch in autumn and spring and give a dressing of balanced general fertilizer in spring. The plant needs careful staking for it can otherwise become an untidy mess; wrap-around supports or twiggy branches are most effective. Cut back above-

Right: *Musk mallow flower.*
Left: *White musk mallow (*Malva moschata*) 'Alba'.*

ground growth in autumn. Most easily propagated from seed sown in late spring in pots of soil-based compost in a cold-frame.

Musk Mallow Basics
Problems: Rust.

Recommended Varieties: The normal species has pink flowers but there is definitely much to recommend the beautiful white-flowered 'Alba'.

Ornamental Appeal: Pink or white, single, rather saucer-shaped flowers for long periods in summer, with large, finely divided, almost feathery foliage.

Site and Soil: Full sun or very light shade; rich and free-draining soil.

Hardiness: Very hardy, tolerating −20°C (−4°F) or below.

Size: Will attain about 75cm–1m × 45–60cm (30in–3ft × 18–24in) after two or three years.

Musk Mallow Uses
Culinary The foliage, when young, makes an unexpected and strange-looking vegetable.

Non-Culinary The best known and most important of several old medicinal uses was the preparation of a cough remedy from the roots.

Marrubium vulgare

Horehound

It's fortunate that the horehound has a good herbal pedigree for it is a most unprepossessing thing that, otherwise, would be unlikely to gain garden room anywhere. An herbaceous perennial, it has been cultivated since antiquity as a cough remedy and even today,

proprietary preparations include extracts of it. The unusual English name probably derives from the same source as 'hoary', meaning 'with greyish hair'.

Cultivation and Care

Mulch horehound in autumn and spring, giving a dressing of balanced general fertilizer in spring. Cut down above-ground growth in autumn. Propagate by division or by seed sown in late spring in soil-based compost in a cold-frame.

Horehound Basics

Problems: None.

Recommended Varieties: The normal species only is available.

Ornamental Appeal: Very little, small rather misshapen and woolly leaves with tiny white, labiate flowers in clusters on the stem in summer.

Site and Soil: Full sun and shelter, in a light, very free-draining soil.

Hardiness: Very hardy, tolerating −20°C (−4°F) or below.

Size: Will attain about 45 × 25cm (18 × 10in) after two or three years.

Above: *Horehound foliage.*
Left: *Horehound (*Marrubium vulgare*).*

Horehound Uses

Culinary None.

Non-Culinary Cough remedies, expectorants and general cold cures are prepared from the woolly leaves.

Melilotus officinalis

Melilot, Sweet Clover

You are more likely to find melilot in farming than gardening books as it was, in the past, an important fodder crop and has never really played a significant part in modern gardens. This is both surprising and unfortunate for it is a species with important herbal uses and a most attractive appearance. The name derives from an old word for honey, an allusion both to the plant's perfume and its value as a honey plant. It is now becoming fairly generally available at herb nurseries and, hopefully, will become more widely grown.

Cultivation and Care

Grow as a biennial, sowing *in situ* in late spring for flowering the following year. It may also be raised in pots in a cold-frame for planting out in the following spring if space is limited.

Melilot Basics

Problems: None.

Recommended Varieties: Normal species is the only form available.

MELILOTUS OFFICINALIS · MELILOT, SWEET CLOVER

Far left and left:
Melilot
*(*Melilotus officinalis*).*

Ornamental Appeal: Slender spikes of tiny, yellow, honey-scented, pea flowers for long periods in summer and rather dainty, clover-like foliage.

Site and Soil: Full sun or very light shade, in light but fairly rich and free-draining soil.

Hardiness: Very hardy, tolerating −20°C (−4°F) or below.

Size: Will attain about 75cm–1m × 50cm (30in–3ft × 20in) within its two year span.

Melilot Uses

Culinary Leaves are used to add flavour to stuffings. They may also be used with cheese; a related species is used in Switzerland to flavour Gruyère.

Non-Culinary Various minor medicinal uses: an extract from the flowers has been used to produce an eyewash, although this should never be done without professional supervision; and leaf extracts have been used to produce an inflammation-reducing poultice.

Melissa officinalis

Lemon Balm

For some reason, a great many herbs are lemon scented; this one probably more than most. In its variegated form, and in the spring, this is among the most beautiful of all herb plants and it deserves a place in any herb garden. The only real pity is that this herbaceous perennial does become a little straggly and unkempt as summer wears on; and it is invasive. There's no doubt that the herbal virtues of the species have been known since ancient times.

Cultivation and Care

Mulch lightly in autumn and spring and give a balanced general fertilizer in spring. Cut down all top growth to just above the soil level in autumn.

Propagate from semi-ripe cuttings in summer; may also be successful by division if the plants aren't too old and woody.

Lemon Balm Basics

Problems: Can be invasive.

Recommended Varieties: The normal species, the lovely variegated form 'Aurea' and a less pretty golden-leaved variety 'All Gold' are all widely available.

Ornamental Appeal: More or less heart-shaped, small, fresh green leaves (with a beautiful golden variegation in 'Aurea'), small, lipped, yellowish flowers in summer.

Site and Soil: Full sun or very light shade, in rich, moist but not waterlogged soil.

Hardiness: Very hardy, tolerating −20°C (−4°F) or below.

Size: Will attain about 75cm–1m × 50cm (30in–3ft × 20in) within three years, but this height figure is somewhat deceptive because, in the early part of the season, the plant forms a low and very neat rosette of foliage.

Above: *Lemon balm can be used in herbal tea.*
Left: *Lemon balm (*Melissa officinalis*) 'Aurea'.*

Lemon Balm Uses

Culinary Fresh young leaves in salads, with fish, some meat and cheese dishes and also to add lemon flavour to desserts. One of the more appealing lemon-scented teas can be made from a leaf infusion.

Non-Culinary The tea is said to relieve colds and congestion while a leaf poultice has been used to aid wound healing and give relief from stings.

Mentha spp.

Mint

Mint is one of the most familiar, one of the classic, herb plants, present in almost every garden, whether or not there is a dedicated herb-growing area. Sadly, however, most gardens have but one plant, generally not of the best or most attractive variety; and that plant will have been stuck in a corner from which it has spread outwards to the point of becoming an invasive nuisance. However, with 25 species of perennials (and a few annuals) to choose from, the genus offers an enticing range of delicious colours and fragrances for any garden.

Cultivation and Care

Fill 20cm (8in) plastic pots (with bottoms and drainage holes) with a soil-based compost. Then plant the mints, one per pot and sink the pots almost to the rims in the garden bed. The pots will prevent the runners from spreading into the rest of the garden. In the autumn, lift the pots and trim off any wayward shoots that threaten to escape. Then, every second autumn, remove some small shoots and pot them up separately to produce fresh plants to be used to replace the old ones the following year. You will sometimes see mints for sale as seed but don't waste time with them as the best forms do not come true.

Mint Basics

Problems: None.

Recommended Varieties: Far and away the most common garden mint is spearmint, the mint of chewing gum, but not the best for mint sauce. So take your pick from among the following: *Mentha* x *gracilis* 'Variegata' (ginger mint), golden-flecked leaves, gingery scent, a beauty; *M. longifolia* (horse mint), a large, coarse and unattractive plant with a spearmint scent; *M.* x *piperita* (peppermint), dark green leaves, peppermint taste, the one for summer drinks; *M. p. citrata* (orange or eau de Cologne mint), dark bronze-green foliage and refreshing scent; *M. pulegium* (pennyroyal), small leaves, creeping habit, peppermint scent, 'Upright' is an erect growing form; *M. requienni* (Corsican mint), a tiny gem, minute leaves and flowers, creeping habit, peppermint scent, wonderful for growing in damp crevices between stones; *M. spicata*

Right: *Mint is often used in cocktails, such as this mojito.*
Left: *Peppermint (*Mentha x piperita*).*

Left: *Variegated pineapple mint (*Mentha suaveolens *'Variegata').*
Right: *Mint sauce is a popular condiment for roasted meat, especially lamb.*

(spearmint) is the basic, standard, spearmint-scented plant – have one and use it with potatoes, but don't use it to the exclusion of everything else. 'Crispa' is a robust, pretty, curled leafed variant. *M. suaveolens* (applemint), rounded, woolly leaves and apple scent, the best mint-sauce mint; *M. x villosa alopecuroides* ('Bowles Mint'), large, rounded, hairy, apple-scented leaves, another good one for mint sauce.

Ornamental Appeal: Attractive, fresh-looking leaves, basically green but often with delightful variegations and other patterns; small purple flowers in summer.

Site and Soil: Full sun to light or almost moderate shade; mints are among the most shade-tolerant herbs. They tolerate most soils but will never be successful in dry and impoverished conditions.

Hardiness: Very hardy, tolerating −20°C (−4°F) or below.

Size: Varies greatly with variety from about 1 × 10cm (½ × 4in) in two years for *M. requienni* to 1m × 60cm (3ft × 24in) for *M. longifolia*.

Mint Uses

Culinary Mint sauce is the best known use, together with peppermint in cool drinks and leaf sprigs with potatoes but the delicate flavours may be used with almost any savoury or sweet dish and experimenting is fun. Infusions, especially of peppermint, produce delicious tea. For mint sauce, always scald the leaves after chopping them to release all of the flavour, and be sparing with the vinegar (use malt not wine).

Non-Culinary The refreshing fragrances, either fresh or as infusions, give relief, either real or imagined, from nasal congestion, headaches and other discomforts.

Monarda didyma

Bergamot, Bee Balm, Oswego Tea

Yet another balm (the name is derived from the same source as balsam and simply means 'spicy') but although a member of the same family, Lamiaceae, as lemon balm, this is a very different plant and is one of those herbs that is quite as likely to be seen in the ornamental border. And while lemon balm has the fragrance of lemons, bergamot has the fragrance of oranges. The name 'Oswego tea' alludes to the use of the plant by the North American Oswego Native Americans; a use incidentally taken up by European settlers after the shortage of real tea in 1773.

Left: *Scarlet bee balm (*Monarda didyma*) in bloom.* **Right:** *Oswego (bee balm) tea.*

Cultivation and Care

Mulch lightly in autumn and spring and give a balanced general fertilizer in spring. Cut down all top growth to just above soil level in the autumn. Propagate this herbaceous perennial from semi-ripe cuttings in summer; also by division.

Bergamot Basics

Problems: None.

Recommended Varieties: The normal species is a good herb plant but if you prefer rather more strikingly coloured flowers, then select 'Cambridge Scarlet' or even the white form 'Alba'.

Ornamental Appeal: Fresh, rather bright green, narrowly elongated leaves and heads of rather spidery, pink, purple, red or white flowers (depending on variety).

Site and Soil: Full sun or light shade, in rich, moist but not waterlogged soil.

Hardiness: Very hardy, tolerating −20°C (−4°F) or below.

Size: Will attain about 75cm–1m × 30cm (30in–3ft × 12in) within three years.

Bergamot Uses

Culinary Flowers or young leaves can be used for a hint of orange in salads, added to desserts or for infusion.

Non-Culinary The tea is claimed to relieve colds, congestion and similar respiratory problems and also flatulence.

Myosotis spp.

Forget-me-not

Everyone knows the forget-me-not as one of the best loved cottage-garden annuals and wild flowers. But as a herb? Surely not. Yet, in many countries, extract of both flowers and leaves has been, and indeed still is used for herbal purposes. In general, the perennial species have been used most, one of the main drawbacks with the annuals being that they are martyrs to mildew as the summer wears on. But any excuse to grow at least some of these delightful little blue-flowered plants as the edging to a herb garden is to be welcomed.

Cultivation and Care

Sow annuals *in situ* and they will then self-seed year after year. Perennials scarcely need mulching but should be given a balanced general fertilizer in the spring and cut back to soil level

Left: *Forget-me-not flowers (*Myosotis sylvatica*).*
Right: Myosotis *flower essence.*

as soon as mildew takes over in the latter part of the summer. Propagate perennials by seed sown in late spring *in situ* or by division.

Forget-me-not Basics

Problems: Mildew.

Recommended Varieties: There are many annual and perennial species; perhaps the best of the perennials are *Myosotis sylvatica*, *M. alpestris* and *M. scorpioides*. The annual of which you are most likely to obtain seeds is *M. arvensis*; but do avoid those cultivated selections with flowers in any colour other than blue.

Ornamental Appeal: Small, narrowly elongated leaves and masses of familiar tiny bright blue flowers.

Site and Soil: Full sun or light shade; tolerates most soils if not too dry but ideally, light but fairly rich and free-draining.

Hardiness: Very hardy, tolerating −20°C (−4°F) or below.

Size: Varies with species but annuals will attain about 25 × 25cm (10 × 10in) within the year and perennials approximately 30 × 30cm (12 × 12in) after two or three years.

Forget-me-not Uses

Culinary None.

Non-Culinary Leaf and flower extracts are used to treat lung complaints (remember that *Myosotis* is closely related to *Pulmonaria*, lungwort, see page 214).

Myrrhis odorata

Sweet Cicely, Anise

You could be forgiven for thinking that *Myrrhis* is the biblical myrrh but you would be wrong, although the name, from an original Arabic word for an aromatic plant, clearly has the same source. This is one of

the prettiest of the herb umbellifers. Its fresh green leaves are among the earliest growths to thrust upwards from the bare soil of the herb garden in early spring; and it has the advantage over many umbellifers, quite apart from its herbal uses, that it is only of a very modest height.

Above: *Dark brown, ripe Sweet Cicely seeds.*
Left: *Sweet Cicely (*Myrrhis odorata*).*

Ornamental Appeal: Fresh, light green, ferny foliage and small umbels of pretty white spring flowers.

Site and Soil: Generally best in light shade, and in rich, moist but fairly free-draining soils.

Hardiness: Very hardy, tolerating −20°C (−4°F) or below.

Size: Will attain around 1m × 45cm (3ft × 18in) within two or three years.

Cultivation and Care

Mulch in autumn and spring, give a balanced general fertilizer in the spring and cut back all above-ground growth to soil level as soon as the foliage dies in the late autumn. Propagate this herbaceous perennial by division of the plants or from seed sown in late spring in a soil-based compost in a cold-frame.

Sweet Cicely Basics

Problems: Mildew.

Recommended Varieties: The normal species is the only one likely to be seen.

Sweet Cicely Uses

Culinary Leaves are used in salads, with cooked vegetables, cooked meat dishes and also with desserts. Seeds can be added to salads and desserts and the roots cooked as a vegetable and served either hot or cold with a vinaigrette dressing.

Non-Culinary Several minor medicinal uses, and to make a ubiquitous 'health-giving tonic'.

Myrtus communis

Myrtle

Myrtle is truly one of the most exquisitely aromatic plants and, as it is not as tender as many believe; given moderate shelter this shrub will thrive in many areas. It is worthy of a place on purely ornamental grounds and, in mild areas, makes a wonderful hedge. But it does have valuable and ancient herbal uses, too.

Cultivation and Care

Mulch in autumn and spring, give a balanced rose or other potash-rich fertilizer. No pruning is necessary although overgrown plants may be clipped in late spring. Propagate by semi-ripe cuttings in late summer, using a soil-based compost in a propagator with some bottom heat.

Myrtle Basics

Problems: None.

Recommended Varieties: There are several named forms, including, inevitably, a double-flowered variant, but for the herb garden, the neater and more compact variety *tarentina* is the best, and it is more hardy.

Ornamental Appeal: Masses of small, dark, evergreen leaves with beautiful, small, rather rose-like, cream-white flowers in summer.

Site and Soil: Full sun with shelter from cold winds; tolerates most soils provided not heavy and waterlogged. A good container plant in a fairly rich soil-based compost.

Hardiness: Fairly to moderately hardy, tolerating −10°C (14°F) or below.

Size: Will attain around 1 × 1m (3 × 3ft) within four or five years.

Above: *Dry myrtle berries, one with seeds exposed.*
Left: *Myrtle (*Myrtus communis*).*

Myrtle Uses

Culinary Sprigs can be used exactly as rosemary is when roasting meat and with the leaves as an ingredient of stuffing, especially with pork or lamb. The flowers may be used with fruit dishes and other desserts.

Non-Culinary Some minor medicinal uses; leaf extracts have wound-healing and antiseptic properties.

Nepeta cataria

Catmint, Catnip

There's no denying that catmint does have a seemingly magnetic attraction for felines. Visually, it doesn't have a tremendous amount going for it, but you should try to find a place in the herb garden for this herbaceous perennial as it has several herbal merits and some rather more persuasive medicinal properties than many species.

Right: *Catmint (Nepeta cataria).*
Opposite: *Fresh, grey-green, heart-shaped leaf sprigs of catmint.*

Cultivation and Care

Mulch lightly in the autumn and early spring (this soon becomes difficult in spring because of its sprawling habit); give a balanced general fertilizer in the spring and cut the plant back to soil level in autumn.

Catmint Basics

Problems: Attracts cats.

Recommended Varieties: There are numerous species of *Nepeta*, used for a wide number of garden purposes, but the best, basic catmint is the species *N. cataria*.

Ornamental Appeal: Not great, although the mass of greyish-green leaves and small, bluish-purple flowers are rather attractive during the summer – and until the cat rolls on them.

Site and Soil: Full sun; tolerates most soils if not too dry and not heavy and wet.

Hardiness: Very hardy, tolerating −20°C (−4°F) or below.

Size: Will attain around 75 × 30cm (30 × 12in) after about three years.

Catmint Uses

Culinary Fresh leaves can be used when cooking meat, especially lamb, to add a slight mint-like flavour. Also makes a tea of tolerable taste.

Non-Culinary Extracts of leaves and flowers are used to make a cold remedy, probably with some efficacy as the foliage especially has a high vitamin C content.

Ocimum basilicum

Basil

Basil in small pots has now become such an accepted component of supermarket herb counters that fewer gardeners are growing it fresh from seed. However, it really is simplicity to grow yourself, and so much cheaper too. It is always grown as an annual although it can be a short-lived perennial but, as it is tender, it will only survive cold weather in a greenhouse or on a kitchen window ledge. But whether indoors or, perhaps best of all, in small terracotta pots outside, basil has such a fresh fragrance and taste that few can garden or cook without it.

Cultivation and Care

Sow as an annual in early spring, preferably in a propagator with some bottom heat. Occasional clipping in the summer will keep the plants neat.

Basil Basics

Problems: None.

Recommended Varieties: Among several variants are *citriodorum*, with a lemon scent; *purpurascens*, with dark red-purple leaves (which looks attractive when combined with the plain green-leaved form); and *minimum*, the so-called Greek basil, with tiny leaves and a pretty, bushy habit but rather less flavour.

Ornamental Appeal: More or less oval, green leaves (but smaller and/or coloured in some forms) and tiny white or pinkish flowers in the summer.

Site and Soil: Full sun; prefers fairly rich, free-draining soils but it fares best in small pots of loam-based compost.

Hardiness: Barely hardy, tolerating no less than −5°C (23°F).

Size: Will normally attain around 25 × 10cm (10 × 4in) within the season.

Left: *Pesto sauce made with fresh basil.*
Opposite: *Basil (*Ocimum basilicum*).*

Basil Uses

Culinary Fresh leaves are used with salads; they are especially effective when chopped and added with oil and vinegar to tomatoes. It is much used in Italian and Greek cooking and is a major contributor to that much-loved 'Mediterranean' flavour.

Non-Culinary Some minor medicinal applications and widely used in aromatherapy.

Oenothera biennis

Evening Primrose

You can't ignore evening primrose in a herb garden, even if you do have to stay up late to appreciate the best of their blooms. Yes, they are evening plants but they aren't primroses, being in the same family

as the willowherbs. All species of *Oenothera* originated in the New World (although they are now naturalized in many other places too) and the native peoples of North America used them extensively. Wisely too, for the herbal properties are now known to have a sound biochemical basis.

Left: *Evening primrose* (Oenothera biennis*).*
Right: *Evening primrose oil capsules.*

Cultivation and Care

Grow as a biennial, sowing *in situ* in late spring. Once established, will generally self-seed fairly freely.

Evening Primrose Basics

Problems: None.

Recommended Varieties: Among the numerous species, *Oenothera biennis* is the best and easiest for herbal use.

Ornamental Appeal: Saucer-like, bright yellow flowers that tend to open late in the day atop tall stems with bright green, narrowly elongated leaves.

Site and Soil: Full sun, in fairly rich, free-draining soils and intolerant of wet, heavy and cold clays.

Hardiness: Very hardy, tolerating −20°C (−4°F).

Size: Depending on growing conditions, will attain 1– 2m × 45cm (3– 7ft × 18in) within the two seasons.

Evening Primrose Uses

Culinary Roots, stems and leaves can be cooked as vegetables.

Non-Culinary Much used medicinally, mainly for blood-associated conditions such as reducing the likelihood of blood clotting. Also used as a treatment for degenerative diseases, menopausal and other female conditions.

Onobrychis viciifolia

Sainfoin

The name *viciifolia* means 'having leaves like a *Vicia.*' And, as vicias are the vetches, and placed in the same family near to *Onobrychis*, this is hardly surprising. This is another of those members of the pea family that appears to be of more interest from an agricultural than a horticultural standpoint, being an important fodder crop. And yet sainfoin is a plant with a long and fascinating herbal history and it has recently been suggested, with sound evidence, unlike many such suggestions, that it is the sole remaining, unidentified plant of the group of sacred herbs referred to in an 11th-century Anglo-Saxon herbal.

Left: *Sainfoin (Onobrychis viciifolia).*
Right: *Sainfoin flowers.*

Cultivation and Care

Give a very light dressing of bone meal in the spring; cut back above-ground growth hard in autumn. An herbaceous perennial, it is best propagated from seed sown in spring in pots of an soil-based compost in a cold-frame.

Sainfoin Basics

Problems: None.

Recommended Varieties: Normal species only is available.

Ornamental Appeal: Spikes of rather pretty, rose-pink flowers and the familiar, much-divided foliage of vetches and so many other plants of the pea family.

Site and Soil: Full sun; always best in dryish, well-drained but moderately rich soils.

Hardiness: Very hardy, tolerating −20°C (−4°F) or below.

Size: Will attain around 50–75 × 30cm (20–30 × 12in) within two years.

Sainfoin Uses

Culinary Both the young shoots and the leaves may be used in various salads.

Non-Culinary Numerous minor medicinal merits were attached to this plant in earlier times but none seems to have survived to the present day.

Onopordum acanthium

Cotton Thistle

You won't miss an *Onopordum* in the herb garden, or anywhere else for that matter for it is truly a giant among herbaceous plants, and achieves this stature within two seasons. It is a close relative of the familiar, wild, weed thistles and this species is now generally reckoned to be the source of the original thistle emblem of Scotland. It has a good enough herbal pedigree, both culinary and medicinal, but its size is an undeniable drawback to it being planted in the average herb garden.

Cultivation and Care

Sow seed of this biennial in pots of soil-based compost in late spring and then plant out into their growing positions in the early autumn.

Cotton Thistle Basics

Problems: None.

Recommended Varieties: Normal species only is available.

Right: *Cotton thistle (*Onopordum acanthium*). White, fluffy thistledown enables seeds to be blown by the wind.*

Right: *Purple cotton thistle (*Onopordum acanthium*) flowers.*

Ornamental Appeal: The overall size is impressive, as is the contrast between the rich purple of the flowers and the white woolly covering to the remainder of the plant.

Site and Soil: Full sun or very light shade; tolerates most soils but best in rich, fairly well-drained sites.

Hardiness: Very hardy, tolerating −20°C (−4°F) or below.

Size: Will attain around 2 × 1.2– 1.5m (7 × 4– 5ft) in favourable conditions.

Cotton Thistle Uses

Culinary Unopened flowers may be cooked in exactly the same way as globe artichokes although they have even less edible matter and so you may be forgiven for wondering if it is worthwhile. The young stems may also be cooked and eaten.

Non-Culinary Several historical minor medicinal uses but apparently no longer used today.

Origanum spp.

Marjoram and Oregano

There is a handful of truly indispensable herbs and these plants are among them, both for their culinary value, their visual appeal in flower and leaf, and their value as bee plants. *Origanum* is a big genus of largely Mediterranean species in the family Lamiaceae. They are all similar but differ to some degree in colour, habit and aroma.

Cultivation and Care

Mulching is scarcely practical but plants should be give a light dressing of bone meal in spring and the plants cut back hard to soil level in autumn. These herbaceous perennials should be clipped back hard in early spring and are best propagated by semi-ripe cuttings in late summer, rooted in any soil-based compost. Some varieties will also usefully form layers. The best forms do not come true from seed.

Marjoram and Oregano Basics
Problems: None.

Recommended Varieties: *Origanum vulgare* (oregano or, sometimes, wild marjoram) is an untidy plant in its native form with white or pink flowers and a peppery fragrance and flavour;

the beautiful golden-leaved form 'Aureum' with a milder flavour is the prettiest plant in the genus but other good varieties include the variegated

'Gold Tip', 'Compactum', with a neat, cushion habit and darker leaves, and 'Album', with white flowers. *O. marjorana* (sweet marjoram) is less hardy with white flowers.

Ornamental Appeal: Delicate leaves, in varying shades of green or gold; small white or purplish flowers which are very attractive to bees.

Site and Soil: Full sun or very light shade (the golden-leaved forms will scorch in full sun); tolerates most soils but best in rich, well-drained sites.

Hardiness: Generally very hardy, tolerating −20°C (−4°F) or below, although some forms are only fairly hardy, tolerating no less than −5°C (23°F).

Size: Varies with variety but most will attain 20–45 × 20–30cm (8–18 × 8–12in) after two years.

Above: *Fresh oregano.*
Left: *Oregano (*Origanum vulgare*).*

Marjoram and Oregano Uses

Culinary A very wide range of flavouring uses; the leaves are used in salads, stuffings, with cooked meat (chicken especially), fish, egg and cheese; almost any kitchen use is worth the experimentation. An infusion can be made from leaves and flowers to produce an aromatic tea.

Non-Culinary The infusions, both of marjoram and oregano, have been claimed to cure virtually all ailments known to humankind.

199

Papaver spp.

Poppy

After dandelions and daisies, poppies must rank very high on the list of immediately recognizable flowers. And although the use of modern farm weedkillers means that the wild, annual, red field poppy is no longer as familiar as once it was, its extremely long-lived seeds means that it will still germinate and grow in disturbed soil, many years after the flowers were last seen. The poppy genus *Papaver* includes several other species too, and although the perennials have no herbal interest, the fact that one of the annuals has some herbal or medicinal attraction can't have escaped many people. Wars have been fought over the product of the opium poppy and that must be treated with circumspection.

Above: *Field poppies (*Papaver rhoeas*).*
Right: *Poppy seeds and poppy heads.*

Cultivation and Care

Grow as a hardy annual, sowing seeds *in situ* in spring. Given a reasonably large area in which to grow, the singles will self-seed reliably year after year.

Poppy Basics

Problems: Aphids, powdery mildew and a downy mildew.

Recommended Varieties: *Papaver rhoeas* (field poppy), single red flowers with black centre. Derived from it are many garden variants, most notably the Shirley poppies, with single or double flowers and a range of colours including red, pink and white, but never lilac or yellow. *P. somniferum* (opium poppy), a southern European and Asian species with white, lilac or purple flowers, sometimes double.

Ornamental Appeal: Single or double flowers in a range of colours from white to dark purple and red, depending on species and variety. The foliage is of little interest although the waxy, glaucous leaves and stem of *P. somniferum* are an excellent foil for the papery flowers.

Site and Soil: Full sun; always best in well drained but rather rich soils although field poppies are often found naturally on heavier sites too.

Hardiness: Very hardy, tolerating −20°C (−4°F) or below.

Size: Will attain around 75cm– 1m × 20cm (30in– 3ft × 8in) within the season.

Poppy Uses

Culinary The seeds of both the field poppy and opium poppy are used in bread and confectionery. The best seeds are those of the opium poppy, but it must be stressed that only the fully ripe seeds can be used; immature seeds are toxic.

Non-Culinary Field poppy, none, and the only parts of the opium poppy that are not potentially dangerous are the ripe seeds. It is from the unripe seed capsule that the latex is extracted from which raw opium, morphine, codeine and heroin are obtained but the danger of experimenting with these substances cannot be over-stressed and in many countries, the growing of opium poppies is legally restricted.

Pelargonium spp.

Scented Pelargonium

There has long been some confusion between pelargoniums and geraniums: at its simplest, geraniums are hardy and pelargoniums are tender. It may seem curious, therefore, that a group of pelargoniums find themselves in a book that is essentially about hardy plants. In addition, the pelargoniums that are included are those tender perennials that are generally grown as house or greenhouse plants.

Cultivation and Care

Need greenhouse or other protection in winter. Liquid feed with fertilizer high in potash during the growing season, especially if in pots. Dead head regularly. Propagate by softwood cuttings in late summer or early spring; most types root with consummate ease.

Scented Pelargonium Basics

Problems: Aphids, caterpillars.

Recommended Varieties:

There are so many varieties with different scents and also so many varieties with a similar scent but different flowers and foliage that this selection is inevitably limited. The sticky-leaved 'Filicifolium' variety

crops up frequently in catalogues but is slightly poisonous so should be avoided for herbal purposes. The following lists indicate the fragrance first and then other notable

Above: *Pelargonium essential oil.*
Left: *Oakleaf Geranium*
(Pelargonium quercifolium).

features. Clearly some fragrances are more welcome in cooking than others (cedar-flavoured salads aren't to everyone's taste) but they are included for their general appeal.

'Attar of Roses', roses, pink flowers; 'Chocolate Tomentosum', peppermint, brown leaf blotches; 'Citriodorum', citrus, small lilac flowers; 'Clorinda', cedar, large, pink flowers; 'Copthorne', cedar, purple flowers; 'Fragrans', pine, tiny white flowers; 'Graveolens', lemon, the best-known scented variety and the source of oil of geranium; 'Joy Lucille', peppermint, tiny white and mauve flowers; 'Lady Mary', nutmeg, lilac flowers; 'Lady Plymouth', lemon, the variegated-leaf form of 'Graveolens' almost as well known; 'Lilian Pottinger', pine, tiny

white flowers and delightful soft leaves; 'Royal Oak', spicy, incense, mauve flowers.

Ornamental Appeal: Generally small flowers in white, pink or purple or mauve shades, usually very pretty and delicate foliage with varying degrees of indentation, with some variegated.

Site and Soil: Best in pots of soil-based compost.

Hardiness: Barely hardy, tolerating no less than −5°C (23°F).

Size: Varies with species but most will attain around 30 × 25cm (12 × 10in) within the first season from a cutting.

Scented Pelargonium Uses

Culinary Flowers or leaves are used in salads and with cakes or other confectionery or, indeed, as you like.

Non-Culinary Extracted oils are used in aromatherapy.

Petroselinum crispum

Parsley

Everyone knows parsley and many people know at least some of the legends attached to it: that when it grows well, for instance, this indicates that the lady of the house is the dominant partner. Many people know, too, that it can be fickle and very often doesn't germinate easily, and some realize that it is biennial and will die away after two years. There are even those who are aware that there are different forms of parsley, of quite distinct appearance and flavour. But whether you know a great deal or nothing about this plant, there is no denying its value and usefulness in the kitchen.

Cultivation and Care

Grow as a biennial, either sowing *in situ* or in small pots in the greenhouse and then plant it out with the minimum of disturbance. Germination can be very slow and erratic; sow parsley thickly in rows about 25cm (10in) apart and, unless the soil is already at least neutral, add a little lime to the seed drill. Pouring boiling water over the drill is also said to be very effective in removing potential germination inhibitors but it may still fail in an acid soil. Parsley is also successful in pots provided the compost is not allowed to dry out totally.

Above: *Parsley (*Petroselinum crispum *'Moss Curled').*
Right: *Fresh broad-leaved parsley.*

Parsley Basics

Problems: Carrot fly, root aphid, virus.

Recommended Varieties: Any parsley with 'Moss', 'Curled' or similar words in its name will be of rather neat, compact, dark green appearance with tightly curled leaves and a moderate flavour. Italian parsley is a more vigorous, upright plant with a fine flavour and flat, not curled leaves.

Ornamental Appeal: Much-divided and often curled leaves; with many varieties in the darkest and most lush shade of green you are likely to see.

Site and Soil: Full sun or very light shade in rich, well-drained and preferably slightly alkaline soil.

Hardiness: Very hardy, tolerating −20°C (−4°F) or below.

Size: 'Moss Curled' types will attain 15–20 × 15–20cm (6–8 × 6–8in) within the two seasons. More vigorous varieties may be as tall as 60cm (24in) (and of course, all varieties will be much taller if they are left to flower in the second season).

Parsley Uses

Culinary A multitude of uses; it is a great pity when it is used merely as a garnish. Use chopped leaves in sauces, soups, with cold meat, fish and cheese dishes, with cooked vegetables and in salads. And always eat parsley garnish; it's too good to waste.

Non-Culinary As with so many other herbs, an infusion can be made from the leaves and is said to be good for you. Eating fresh parsley will disperse the smell of onions or garlic from the breath.

Pimpinella anisum

Aniseed

A great many umbelliferous herbs smell and taste of aniseed, but this one is the real thing. And yet, ironically, it is grown far less than many of the others. One reason is that it is an annual, but the other is probably that in colder climate gardens, most summers are not long and hot enough for the seeds to ripen fully. It is the seeds that are the principal source of the flavour.

Cultivation and Care

Sow *in situ* in growing positions in spring. It is a fairly small plant and a group will probably be needed, so thin to a spacing of about 15– 20cm (6– 8in) each way.

Aniseed Basics
Problems: None.

Recommended Varieties:
Normal species only is available.

Left: *Aniseed (*Pimpinella anisum*).
Right: *Aniseed seeds.

Ornamental Appeal: Small, bright green, strawberry-like lower leaves with very finely divided upper ones. Tiny white summer flowers in rather loose umbels.

Site and Soil: Full sun or very light shade with shelter from cold winds, in rich, well-drained and slightly alkaline soil.

Hardiness: Barely hardy, tolerating no less than −5°C (23°F).

Size: Will attain around 45 × 25cm (18 × 10in) within a season.

Aniseed Uses

Culinary Seeds add sweetness to confectionery, cheese, meat and pickles and flavour several alcoholic drinks. Flowers and leaves in salads, and roots can be added sparingly to flavour soups.

Non-Culinary Used to relieve chest infections and increase milk production when breast feeding.

Polygonum bistorta

Bistort

Polygonum is a big genus, and most of its members are weeds. Many of those sold as ornamental herbaceous plants are unadventurous in flower and die down in autumn. This one does have herbal properties and so can't be excluded. It is rather less invasive than some of its kin and adaptable to shady spots.

Cultivation and Care

Trim back above-ground growth in autumn, although in mild areas it will form a more or less evergreen mat. To prevent it from becoming invasive, this herbaceous perennial should be lifted and divided every two or three years. Mulch, if practical,

in autumn and spring and give a balanced fertilizer in spring. Propagate by division or by removal of naturally rooted runners, or seed sown in late spring in pots of soil-based compost in a cold-frame.

Bistort Basics

Problems: None.

Recommended Varieties: Normal species is most appropriate for the herb garden.

Ornamental Appeal: Tiny pink flowers in dense club-like spikes in summer, narrowly triangular leaves.

Site and Soil: Full sun to moderate shade in fairly rich, moist and even wet soil, preferably acidic.

Hardiness: Very hardy, tolerating −20°C (−4°F).

Size: Will attain around 1m × 30cm (3ft × 12in) within about two years.

Above: *Bistort flower spike.*
Left: *Common Bistort* (Polygonum bistorta*).*

Bistort Uses

Culinary Young leaves in salads.
Non-Culinary Root extract as an astringent; also used in mouthwash and for cough relief.

Portulaca oleracea

Summer Purslane

This is the summer counterpart to winter purslane (see pages 102–3). It is a half-hardy annual and one with a long history of cultivation in Asia. In consequence, the plant now grown in gardens is a selected form rather than the wild species which is more straggly and too thin-leaved to be of much value. The so-called kitchen garden purslane is a more succulent plant, easily mistaken for a sedum. Some coloured-leaved varieties make good edging plants.

Above: *Purslane (*Portulaca oleracea*).*
Right: *Purslane and caramelized mushroom salad.*

Cultivation and Care

Grow as a half-hardy annual, sowing *in situ* in late spring with 30cm (12in) between rows and thinning to 10–15cm (4–6in) between plants.

Summer Purslane Basics

Problems: None.

Recommended Varieties: The basic green plant seeds will be called 'Common' or 'Kitchen' purslane, with selected coloured-leaf forms as 'Golden' or 'Yellow'.

Ornamental Appeal: Small, more or less rounded, rather fleshy leaves on fleshy stems with tiny, yellow flowers in summer.

Site and Soil: Full sun or very light shade in moderately rich, well-drained soil.

Hardiness: Barely hardy, tolerating no less than −5°C (23°F).

Size: It will grow to attain about 15 × 25cm (6 × 10in) within the season.

Summer Purslane Uses

Culinary Crisp, fresh leaves can be used in salads but should be eaten in moderation as large amounts may be diuretic. Also cooked in numerous oriental dishes and commonly preserved, pickled in vinegar.

Non-Culinary Minor medicinal uses, capitalizing on the diuretic properties.

Primula spp.

Primrose, Cowslip

There can't be a garden that wouldn't be improved by the addition of primroses and cowslips, but their presence in the herb garden needs some explanation; both species can be eaten in one form or another, and both have old, well-tried medicinal uses. And the pleasure that their flowers bring to the spring garden is an added bonus. But grow the true wild forms (bought, not collected); the clarity and honesty of their yellow flowers have something that no brightly coloured garden primula will ever emulate.

Above: *Common primrose.*

Cultivation and Care

Little needed for these herbaceous perennials once established, apart from a light dressing with a balanced fertilizer in spring although they will benefit from some division every four or five years. Propagate by division or from seed sown on the surface of a light, soil-based compost at a temperature which does not exceed 20°C (68°F).

Primrose and Cowslip Basics

Problems: Leaf miners, virus, vine weevil, root rotting.

Recommended Varieties: *Primula vulgaris* is the primrose, with single,

Hardiness: Very hardy, tolerating −20°C (−4°F).

Size: Attains 10–25cm × 10–15cm (4–10 × 4–6in) after two years.

Left: *Cowslip (*Primula veris*).*

clear yellow flowers, one to each stem; *P. veris*, with nodding heads of many golden-yellow flowers, is the cowslip. Accept no substitutes.

Ornamental Appeal: Too well known to justify repeating but, in addition, both primroses and cowslips have two, rather different appeals; one where there is space to grow them in close-planted masses and the other where they are grown as single specimens. But never be tempted to plant them in rows and ranks; they are too informal for that.

Site and Soil: Primroses thrive in light to almost moderate shade, in rich, even heavy, moisture-retentive soil. Cowslips are best grown in full sun, in light, free-draining, alkaline soil.

Primrose and Cowslip Uses

Culinary Cowslip leaves are good in salads but raw primrose is a little bitter although cooked as a vegetable they are excellent; but you need plenty of primroses to make a square meal. The flowers of both have been used in jams, but again, large numbers are required and scattering a few primrose flowers in a salad is a better way to make the most of them.

Non-Culinary All part of primroses (but not, it seems, cowslips) can be used to make an infusion that brings relief from throat problems, headaches, and is generally very invigorating.

Pulmonaria spp.

Lungwort

Lungwort is one of those herbal remedies the use of which was based on the fact that its foliage resembles lung tissue. Whether or not this has any scientific basis, it is one of the most striking and dependable of spring-flowering perennials. Its one drawback, and it is a feature of all of the species, is that they can become invasive if left to their own devices. But, nonetheless, this is a small price to pay for an excellent plant.

Cultivation and Care

Mulch in autumn after the foliage has been cut back to soil level and again in early spring. Give a balanced general fertilizer in spring. Propagate by division; the best forms do not come true from seed.

Left and right:
Lungwort
(Pulmonaria
officinalis)
in flower.

persistently red flowers. The leaves are attractively spotted in most types but are rough to the touch.

Site and Soil: Light to moderate shade, in fairly rich soil that does not dry out.

Hardiness: Very hardy, tolerating −20°C (−4°F).

Size: Will attain 15– 25 × 30– 45cm (6– 10 × 12– 18in) after three years.

Lungwort Basics
Problems: None.

Recommended Varieties: The commonest and oldest species is *Pulmonaria officinalis* with good varieties in 'Cambridge Blue' and 'Blue Mist'. There are red- and also white-flowered forms too but these seem to lack the genuine charm of pulmonarias. Outside this species, there are fine varieties of *P. saccharata* and also some excellent hybrids, most notably 'Mawson's Blue'.

Ornamental Appeal: Small, bell-shaped flowers that open pink but soon turn to a lovely rich blue in the best forms. Other varieties have white or

Lungwort Uses
Culinary None.

Non-Culinary Apart from the claimed value in the control of lung complaints, lungwort has also been recommended as a cure for diarrhoea.

Reseda luteola

Weld

Weld is one of those plant names, like woad, that is redolent of ancient times, of hairy men in hairy cloth, of long-barrows, megaliths and shifting cultivation. Actually, weld is sometimes called woald but *Reseda* is a different plant from *Isatis*, which produces the blue woad dye. There is a connection, nonetheless, in that the yellow dye from weld was once mixed with the blue of woad to produce a third dye called Saxon green. Both plants have been in use since ancient times

and *Reseda*, while no spectacular thing, offers an unbroken connection with those far-off times and the early days of plant cultivation.

Cultivation and Care

Grow as a biennial, sowing seed *in situ* in late spring or early summer and thinning out plants in autumn to flower in the following year. Once established in appropriate conditions, should self-seed.

Weld Basics

Problems: None.

Left and right: *Weld (*Reseda luteola*).*

Recommended Varieties: Normal species only is available.

Ornamental Appeal: Modest; tall spikes of tiny, pale yellow-green summer flowers and narrowly elongated, waxy leaves.

Site and Soil: Full sun, best in a moderately rich and well-drained soil.

Hardiness: Very hardy, tolerating −20°C (−4°F).

Size: Will attain 75cm– 1.2m × 30cm (30in– 4ft × 12in) within the two seasons.

Weld Uses

Culinary None.

Non-Culinary Source of a bright yellow dye.

Rosmarinus officinalis

Rosemary

Rosemary is among the handful of instantly recognizable herb plants, and is one shrubby species that no herb garden should be without. Unfortunately, there is a general belief that rosemary can be left forever without any need for attention, the consequence being that gardens everywhere contain over-sized, misshapen straggly looking examples of a plant that can be so neat and compact as to form one of the loveliest of small hedges. Yes, grow rosemary, but grow her carefully.

Cultivation and Care

Mulch in autumn and spring and give a balanced general or rose fertilizer in spring. May be clipped to shape, with inevitable loss of some flowers, or pruned by cutting out the oldest third of the branches every spring. Propagate by semi-ripe cuttings in a soil-based compost in a closed, warm propagator in late summer.

Rosemary Basics

Problems: None.

Recommended Varieties: It is important to select varieties with care for they range widely in habit, vigour, flower colour and, to some extent,

Above: *Rosemary (*Rosmarinus officinalis*).*

hardiness. All important garden forms are varieties of the Mediterranean *Rosmarinus officinalis*: *albiflorus*, white flowers; 'Benenden Blue' (also called 'Collingwood Ingram'), pale leaves, blue flowers, slightly citrus-like scent; 'Majorca Pink', pink flowers, less hardy; 'Miss Jessopp's Upright', blue flowers, erect, upright habit; 'Severn Sea' (not 'Seven Seas', which it is sometimes called), deep purple flowers, spreading habit, less hardy; 'Sissinghurst Blue', fine clear blue flowers.

Ornamental Appeal: Very pretty, narrow, almost needle-like green leaves crowded onto the stems with masses of small, usually blue flowers intermingled in summer.

Site and Soil: Full sun; tolerant of a wide range of soils but always best on rich, well-drained, slightly alkaline soil. Intolerant of heavy, wet conditions.

Hardiness: Varies with varieties from fairly hardy, tolerating −5 to −10°C (23 to 14°F), to hardy, tolerating −15°C (5°F).

Size: Varies with variety from about 45 × 45cm (18 × 18in) to 2m × 75cm (7ft × 30in), without pruning.

Above: *Sprig of fresh rosemary.*

Rosemary Uses

Culinary Indispensable; traditionally, of course, sprigs are used to garnish roasting lamb but it is good with other meats too and also chopped (together with the flowers) in salads.

Non-Culinary Uses allied to pain relief and easing discomfort by improvement of blood circulation.

Rubia tinctoria

Madder

This more or less scrambling or climbing herbaceous perennial is one of those rather few dye plants that also has value as a medicinal herb. It isn't a thing of great beauty but as it was once cultivated

widely and achieved very considerable importance, it is well worthy of a spot in larger herb collections and is valuable, as much as anything, because climbing herbs are rare.

Cultivation and Care

Mulch lightly in autumn and spring and cut back to just above soil level in late autumn. Give any balanced general fertilizer in spring. Propagate by semi-ripe cuttings in a soil-based compost in a cold-frame in summer, or by layering or by seed sown in the late spring in a soil-based compost in a cold-frame.

Right: *Dried madder roots.*
Left: *Madder (Rubia tinctoria).*

Madder Basics

Problems: None.

Recommended Varieties: Normal species only is available.

Ornamental Appeal: Scrambling or climbing stems with rather pretty whorls of light green leaves and masses of tiny yellow flowers borne along the stem in summer.

Site and Soil: Full sun to light or almost moderate shade, in free-draining, fairly rich soils; intolerant of heavy conditions.

Hardiness: Hardy to very hardy, tolerating around −15°C (5°F).

Size: Will attain a scrambling mass of about 1 × 1m (3 × 3ft) after two years.

Madder Uses

Culinary None.

Non-Culinary In addition to the roots being the source of the madder dyes in reds and browns, also used to produce a treatment for disorders from urinary malfunction to constipation.

Rumex acetosa

Sorrel

Sorrel soup is not uncommon but many consumers of it are unlikely to know this as the perennial *Rumex*. Nor are they likely to think of *Rumex* as dock, and one of the most pernicious of pernicious weeds. The reality is that while sorrel can become invasive, it will never assume the troublesome level of dock; and sorrel soup is palatable.

Cultivation and Care

Almost none needed once established although its growth will be improved by a little general fertilizer in spring, cutting down the foliage as it browns in the winter and dividing every three

or four years. Propagate by division, by root cuttings or from seed, sown in early summer in a soil-based compost in a cold-frame.

Sorrel Basics

Problems: Fungal leaf spots, leaf-eating insects.

Recommended Varieties: Normal species only is available although a very pretty related species, *Rumex scutatus*, the buckler leaf sorrel with small silvery leaves, with a shape reminiscent of those of the tulip tree, is sometimes offered.

Ornamental Appeal: Not a great deal because there's no denying that the plant *does* look like a small version of a dock with the same elongated leaves and spike of minute pinkish flowers.

Site and Soil: Full sun or moderate shade, in almost any soil although less tolerant of heavy, wet conditions than their weed relatives.

Hardiness: Very hardy, tolerating −20°C (−4°F).

Above: *Sorrel soup.*
Left: *Sorrel (*Rumex acetosa*).*

Size: Will attain 60cm– 1.2m × 30cm (24in– 4ft × 12in) after two or three years.

Sorrel Uses

Culinary Young leaves are used in the aforementioned soup, in salads and also as the basis of a rather peculiar-looking sauce. But use only young leaves as they become very bitter with age.

Non-Culinary An infusion of the leaves is used to treat ulcers and also for urinary complaints.

Ruta graveolens

Rue

Rue is worthy of inclusion in any herb garden for it has a leaf form and a colour that is unusual, if not unique among herb plants. This shrubby perennial also has a very long herbal history and is widely recommended for its culinary virtues and numerous medicinal properties but it is one of the very few garden herbs that must be treated with considerable circumspection for it can cause unpleasant and even dangerous symptoms in some people.

Cultivation and Care

Mulch in autumn and spring and give a balanced general fertilizer in spring. Prune hard in spring, but wait until all winter cold damage has occurred. Propagate by semi-ripe cuttings in summer in a soil-based compost in a cold-frame.

Rue Basics

Problems: None.

Recommended Varieties: The normal species is widely available but two variants are much more attractive: 'Jackman's Blue', a more compact plant with steely-blue foliage, and

Left: *Rue (*Ruta graveolens*).*

'Variegata', with yellowish-cream leaf blotches.

Ornamental Appeal: Finely divided leaves, rather like those of a large maidenhair fern; rather disproportionately small, green-yellow flowers in summer.

Site and Soil: Full sun or light shade; best in moderately rich, well drained alkaline soil.

Hardiness: Hardy, tolerating about −15°C (5°F).

Size: Will attain 50–75 × 30cm (20–30 × 12in) within two years.

Left: *Wine made with rue.*

Rue Uses

Culinary Leaves and seeds are used to give a bitter flavour to sauces and other food dressings, but to be used with caution.

Non-Culinary An infusion of the leaves has long been recommended for the treatment of wounds and various other, blood-related conditions. But it should only be used under expert supervision as the leaves also have insecticidal properties and are particularly dangerous for pregnant women.

Salvia spp.

Sage

A herb garden without sage isn't worthy of the name but it's a shame that so many have so few and that just one plant of one variety is sufficient for most people. There is probably a wider range in leaf colour among the various sages that in any other single group of herb, and while some are less hardy, a representative group should be within the capability of almost all herb gardeners.

Cultivation and Care

Mulch in autumn and spring. Give a balanced general fertilizer in spring. Cut back dead flower heads as flowers fade and prune them hard in spring, cutting back to about 15–20cm (6–8in) above soil level. Propagate these shrubby perennials by semi-ripe cuttings in summer, struck in a soil-based compost in a cold-frame.

Sage Basics

Problems: None.

Recommended Varieties: The hardiest and easiest sages are all varieties of *Salvia officinalis* and, although the basic green-leaved species must be in

your collection, you should also have 'Albiflora', white flowers; a form called simply 'broad-leaved', with, oddly enough, broad leaves; 'Icterina', pale green leaves with gold variegation; 'Purpurascens', deep red-purple

Right: *Purple-leaved sage (*Salvia officinalis *'Purpurascens').*

leaves; 'Purpurascens Variegata', extraordinarily variegated leaves, basically as in 'Purpurascens' but with large, angular areas in pink and cream-white; and 'Tricolor', pale green leaves with pink and white variegation. Related and useful species are *S. sclarea* (clary), with large toothed leaves and more striking flowers, it tends to be biennial in some gardens; *S. elegans* (pineapple-scented sage) a less hardy, but very attractive plant with mint-like leaves.

Above: *Fresh sage leaves.*

Ornamental Appeal: Broadly elongated leaves that are rough textured but offer a wide range of colour variants. Typically labiate, generally bluish-purple flowers produced in summer.

Site and Soil: Full sun, light, free-draining, fairly rich alkaline soil.

Hardiness: Most forms are moderately hardy to very hardy, tolerating between −10 and −20°C (14 and −4°F), depending on the variety.

Size: Differs with variety from about 30– 80 × 30– 45cm (12– 32 × 12– 18in) after two or three years.

Sage Uses

Culinary Sage and onion stuffing is, of course, the best known use of sage and certainly the leaves are valuable with many kinds of cooked meat. The flavour is a little strong for them to be used raw in salads although the flowers can be used, both for flavour and visual appeal.

Non-Culinary Many medicinal uses, an infusion of the leaves especially being valuable in assisting digestion.

Sanguisorba minor

Salad Burnet

Apparently one of Frances Bacons' favourite herbs, the leaves of this easy-to-grow herbaceous perennial have a pleasant light cucumber flavour and smell. Cucumber taste or not, *Sanguisorba* is a pretty little thing and every herb garden should have one.

Above: *Salad Burnet (*Sanguisorba minor*).*

Cultivation and Care

Mulch very lightly, if at all, in spring and give a light dressing of a balanced general fertilizer in spring. Best propagated from seed in late spring in a soil-based compost in a cold-frame.

Salad Burnet Basics

Problems: None.

Recommended Varieties: Normal species only is available.

Ornamental Appeal: Very pretty, almost fern-like, divided and toothed leaves; small globular flower heads in summer.

Site and Soil: Full sun; prefers light, free-draining, alkaline soil.

Hardiness: Very hardy, tolerating −20°C (−4°F).

Size: Will attain about 25–75 × 25cm (10–30 × 10in) within two or three years; those used to seeing it growing wild on hillsides may be surprised by these dimensions but in the wild, it is grazed by sheep.

Above: *Fresh sprigs of Salad Burnet.*

Salad Burnet Uses

Culinary In salads, sauces, soups, stews, casseroles with cooked meats and in summer drinks; indeed anywhere that a cucumber flavour is desirable but the real thing is impractical.

Non-Culinary An infusion of the leaves is recommended for the treatment of haemorrhoids and bowel problems.

Santolina spp.

Cotton lavender

Santolina, cotton lavenders, lavender cottons – you can choose which name you prefer – have become more familiar in recent years as ornamentals rather than herbs. But this plant has a long herb garden history, having originated in the Mediterranean and often used as an edging plant in knot and other formal gardens. Given the right growing conditions, this evergreen shrubby perennial should be in all herb collections.

Cultivation and Care

Mulch lightly in autumn and spring and give a little general fertilizer in spring. Best and neatest when clipped in the spring after any likelihood of further winter cold damage is over. Propagate by semi-ripe cuttings in summer, struck in any soil-based compost in a cold-frame.

Cotton Lavender Basics

Problems: None.

Recommended Varieties: There are several species and many varieties, all equally attractive. The most common and longest in cultivation is *Santolina chamaecyparissus* (in effect, cypress-leaved; also known as *S. incana*) with cheerful, golden-yellow button flowers. Selected forms include 'Lambrook Silver', markedly silvery

Left: *Cotton lavender (*Santolina chamaecyparissus*).*
Right: *Cotton lavender flower and leaves.*

leaves, and 'Lemon Queen', shorter, neater habit with paler flowers. Another common dwarf form is *nana* 'Pretty Carol'. *S. pinnata* has more markedly feathery leaves and, in the sub-species *neapolitana*, these are silvery with particularly well-coloured yellow flowers. 'Edward Bowles' and 'Sulphurea' are selected forms with especially good flower colours. The best of the rest is *S. rosmarinifolia* (with greener, rosemary-like leaves), which is most attractive of all in the variety 'Primrose Gem'.

Ornamental Appeal: Very pretty combination of small yellow flowers and neat, generally greyish or silver-green foliage.

Site and Soil: Full sun in light, free-draining, not very rich but not impoverished soil.

Hardiness: Moderately hardy to hardy, tolerating around −15°C (5°F).

Size: Will attain 30–60 × 30cm (12–24 × 12in) after three years.

Cotton Lavender Uses

Culinary None.

Non-Culinary Various minor medicinal uses, ranging from a treatment for internal parasites to the alleviation of jaundice.

Saponaria officinalis

Soapwort

The best known soapwort in gardens today is the ornamental rock garden species, *Saponaria ocymoides*, but its cultivation history is shorter than that of this one, the real soapwort, and the source of a real and very valuable soap. It belongs to the carnation family, Caryophyllaceae, as its flowers readily betray, and its soap-producing properties were known in ancient times and still find a use today, especially in the cleaning of delicate old fabrics. An herbaceous perennial, it is a choice herb, in its appearance, its use and its history.

Cultivation and Care

Mulch in autumn and spring and give a balanced fertilizer in spring. Cut back dead flower heads as the flowers fade and cut back to just above soil level in autumn. Propagate by semi-

Left: *Soapwort (*Saponaria officinalis*).*
Right: Saponaria officinalis *'Rosea Plena'*.

ripe cuttings in summer, struck in a soil-based compost in a cold-frame or by removal of runner; also sown from seed, in spring in a soil-based compost in a cold-frame.

Soapwort Basics
Problems: Aphids.

Recommended Varieties: The normal species is a fine enough plant but there are selected forms: 'Alba Plena', double white flowers; 'Rosea Plena', double pink flowers; and 'Dazzler', variegated foliage.

Ornamental Appeal: More or less oval, pointed, mid-green leaves in whorls on the stem; single pink, rather carnation-like and fragrant summer flowers.

Site and Soil: Full sun in light, free-draining, fairly rich alkaline soil.

Hardiness: Very hardy, tolerating −20°C (−4°F).

Size: Will attain about 50– 75 × 25cm (20– 30 × 10in) after two or three years.

Soapwort Uses
Culinary Despite its soapy properties, the flowers may be added to salads where they impart a slightly interesting, and not remotely soap-like flavour.

Non-Culinary Used to produce a skin-cleansing preparation, and a soap, extracted in boiling water.

Satureja spp.

Savory

Savory sounds as if it should be a cooking herb although the derivation of the name is different from that of savoury. There are two superficially similar species, similar in flavour but differing in that one is a shrubby perennial and the other an unexpectedly woody annual. Both have been used for centuries, but are among those traditional and useful herbs found relatively infrequently in gardens today. Perhaps it is because they rather resemble their better known relatives, the thymes, and because people have forgotten how best to use them in the kitchen.

Left: *Summer Savory (*Satureja hortensis*).*
Opposite: *Winter Savory (*Satureja montana*).*

Ornamental Appeal: Small, elongated dark green leaves and very small pink or white summer flowers.

Site and Soil: Full sun in light, free-draining, fairly rich alkaline soil.

Hardiness: Moderately hardy to hardy, tolerating around −10 to −15°C (14 to 5°F).

Size: Both species will attain about 30–45 × 25–30cm (12–18 × 10–12in).

Cultivation and Care

Winter savory should be mulched lightly in autumn and spring and given a balanced general fertilizer in spring. Trim lightly in spring after the danger of any winter cold damage is passed. Propagate by semi-ripe cuttings in summer, struck in a soil-based compost in a cold-frame. Grow summer savory as a hardy annual, sowing *in situ* in spring.

Savory Basics
Problems: None.

Recommended Varieties: The perennial winter savory is *Satureja montana*; the annual summer version is *S. hortensis*.

Savory Uses

Culinary Fresh leaves are used to add a peppery flavour to salads and cooked vegetables.

Non-Culinary An infusion is used as an aid to digestion and also a mouth-refreshing gargle.

Scutellaria lateriflora
Skullcap

Eating anything called skullcap can't be an entirely enticing prospect although its ominous name relates to no more than the shape of the flowers. It is not an exciting species, and is yet another member of the huge family Lamiaceae with some herbal properties. *Scutellaria* itself is indeed a large genus – of which this fairly widely available species

is just one – and many of its species have some herbal attributes.

Cultivation and Care

Mulch in autumn and spring and give a balanced general fertilizer in spring. Cut back to soil level in late autumn and divide every three or four years. Propagate this herbaceous perennial by division or from semi-ripe cuttings in summer, struck in a soil-based compost in a cold-frame.

Left: *Skullcap*
(Scutellaria lateriflora).

Left: *Dried skullcap as used in infusions.*

Skullcap Basics

Problems: None.

Recommended Varieties: Normal species only is available but there are related and similar forms, including the *Scutellaria galericulata* and *S. minor.*

Ornamental Appeal: Modest; small blue, typical, lipped labiate flowers in summer on a tall, branched plant with rather coarse, toothed leaves.

Site and Soil: Full sun to light or almost moderate shade; tolerates most soils provided not very heavy or waterlogged.

Hardiness: Very hardy, tolerating −20°C (−4°F).

Size: Will attain about 75cm–1m × 45cm (30in–3ft × 18in) after three years.

Skullcap Uses

Culinary None.

Non-Culinary Many minor medicinal uses, especially an infusion of the leaves, used, among other things as a treatment for hysteria.

Sempervivum tectorum

Houseleek

House because they grow on house roofs; leek because someone with exceptionally bad eyesight must have once thought they detected a resemblance; and *Sempervivum* because they live for a very long time and someone else must have believed that they live forever. The houseleeks must be among the most familiar of all succulents and yet it remains a surprise to many to realize that they have herbal value and, indeed, the original reason that they were cultivated (and presumably spread from gardens to roofs) was for precisely this reason. Subsequently, they were deliberately planted on houses for the fanciful belief that they would protect them from natural disasters, such as lightning.

Left: *Common houseleek (*Sempervivum tectorum*).*
Right: *Close-up of a houseleek.*

Cultivation and Care

Apart from a very light dressing with bonemeal in spring, none necessary. An herbaceous perennial, it can be propagated by the removal of off-sets in the spring.

Houseleek Basics

Problems: None.

Recommended Varieties: There are numerous species of *Sempervivum* but *S. tectorum* is the original one of myth and legend.

Ornamental Appeal: Striking rosettes of very fleshy, green, pink-tipped leaves. A stout spike of rich pink flowers may be produced in summer.

Site and Soil: It's not necessary to plant houseleeks on your roof and any site in full sun and a light free-draining, preferably impoverished soil is ideal.

Hardiness: Very hardy, tolerating −20°C (−4°F).

Size: Will attain about 8–10 × 15–20cm (3½–4 × 6–8in) after two or three years.

Houseleek Uses

Culinary Has been used in cooking and fresh in salads but the flavour is astringent.

Non-Culinary Sap from the fresh leaves has both soothing and healing properties when applied to rashes, bites, stings and any other skin abrasions.

Sesamum indicum

Sesame

There are probably few plant products so well known yet of such obscure origin as sesame seeds. There are two probable reasons for this: first, sesame seeds can be bought so readily and thus there is no need to grow your own; and second, the seeds of this tender annual will only ripen in warm seasons. But that is no reason not to include it for it is strikingly different from anything else you are likely to have in your herb garden.

Cultivation and Care

Raise in the same way as corn, sowing the seeds in the spring in a heated greenhouse, hardening-off the young plants and then planting them out when the danger of the last frost has passed.

Sesame Basics

Problems: None.

Right: *Flower of the sesame (*Sesamum indicum*).*

Recommended Varieties: Normal species only is available, if you are lucky and can obtain fresh seed that hasn't been killed in the drying process.

Above: *Sesame seeds.*

Ornamental Appeal: Tall, rather cereal-like plants with broad, spreading leaves and trumpet-shaped, purplish-white flowers. The seeds are formed, in warm conditions, in elongated upright pods.

Site and Soil: Full sun, in a warm sheltered situation and good, rich, free-draining soils.

Hardiness: Barely hardy, tolerating no less than about −5°C (23°F).

Size: In good conditions, will attain 1.5– 2m × 75cm (5– 7ft × 30in) in the season.

Sesame Uses

Culinary Add the seeds to both sweet and savoury dishes to impart a delicious, rather nutty flavour and crunchy texture. In oriental cooking, the seeds are also crushed to produce a paste that is widely used.

Non-Culinary Various medical benefits have been claimed for the seeds, especially associated with urinary problems

Sium sisarum

Skirret, Crummock

This is an interesting herb, being one of the few herbal umbellifers not to have originated in Western Europe or the Mediterranean. It is an Eastern European species that was grown extensively by the Romans who took it, like so many other plants, to all corners of their empire, although it isn't known when the swollen-rooted form originated.

Cultivation and Care

Mulch in autumn and spring and cut down the above-ground growth in autumn. Give a balanced general fertilizer in spring. Propagate this herbaceous perennial by division or from seed, sown in late spring in a soil-based compost in a cold-frame.

Skirret Basics

Problems: None.

Recommended Varieties: There are several species of *Sium* but *S. sisarum* is the one to choose.

Ornamental Appeal: Tall, and typically umbelliferous with umbels of tiny white flowers and divided leaves, less divided than those of many other species.

Above: *Edible skirret roots.*
Left: *Skirret (*Sium sisarum*).*

Skirret Uses

Culinary The swollen roots are cooked and eaten in much the same way as Jerusalem artichokes. The young shoots are said also to be tasty when cooked.

Non-Culinary There are a number of fairly vague recommendations in herbal lore for the use of the roots and stems for the enhancement of general well-being.

Site and Soil: Full sun or light shade; tolerates most soils but best in rich alkaline loam.

Hardiness: Very hardy, tolerating −20°C (−4°F).

Size: Will attain 1.2– 1.5m × 75cm (4– 5ft × 30in) in two or three years.

Smyrnium olusatrum

Alexanders

If you don't live near to the sea, you could be forgiven for not knowing that umbellifers can have yellow flowers. So many species are white with feathery foliage, that coming across this one with yellow umbels and large, barely divided leaves, in its natural habitat, seldom far from the coast, is always a delightful surprise. This herbaceous perennial isn't named after Alexander the Great, at least not directly, for its name seems to be a reference to the city of Alexandria and an allusion, therefore, to its considerable importance to Mediterranean peoples.

Cultivation and Care

Mulch in autumn and spring and give a balanced general fertilizer in spring. Cut down above-ground growth in the autumn. Propagate by division or from seed sown in a soil-based compost in a cold-frame in early summer.

Alexanders Basics

Problems: None.

Recommended Varieties: Normal species only is available.

Ornamental Appeal: The combination of yellow flower heads and pale lime-green leaves is striking.

Site and Soil: Full sun to moderate shade in preferably fairly rich and moist but not waterlogged soil.

Hardiness: Moderately hardy, tolerating −15°C (5°F).

Size: Will attain about 90cm– 1.2m × 60cm (34in– 4ft × 24in) in two years.

Left and right: *Alexanders* (*Smyrnium olusatrum*).

Alexanders Uses

Culinary Many and varied uses: the young leaves in salads, the young shoots cooked as a vegetable, the roots boiled like a parsnip or Hamburg parsley, the flowers in salads, the seeds as a peppery flavouring. The seeds have even been used, ground, as a pepper substitute during times of shortage.

Non-Culinary None.

Stachys officinalis

Betony

There are several different plants called betony, also sometimes known as hedgenettle, none of them strikingly attractive but all have some other interest. In the case of *Stachys officinalis*, that interest is herbal and this herbaceous perennial has long been used for a wide range of medicinal purposes. It was also used extensively in country districts as a readily available substitute for tobacco, a use that was revived during the Second World War when the real thing was hard to come by.

Left: *Wood betony (Stachys officinalis).*
Right: *Purple betony flowers.*

Cultivation and Care

Mulch lightly in autumn and spring and give a balanced general fertilizer in spring. Cut down above-ground growth in autumn. Propagate by division or from the seed sown in a soil-based compost in a cold-frame in early summer.

Betony Basics

Problems: None.

Recommended Varieties: The normal species is widely available but two very predictable selected variants are 'Alba' with white flowers and 'Rosea Plena' with double pink ones.

Ornamental Appeal: Not a great deal to become excited about: bright pink, lipped flowers on a tall stem with rather roughly toothed leaves; a bit like a stretched-out dead nettle.

Site and Soil: Full sun to moderate shade in preferably fairly rich and moist but not waterlogged soil.

Hardiness: Very hardy, tolerating −20°C (−4°F).

Size: Will attain 60cm–1m × 30–45cm (24in–3ft × 12–18in) in two years.

Betony Uses

Culinary None.

Non-Culinary Apart from being smoked, betony leaves have been used to make preparations with various beneficial, blood-related properties such as wound healing, as well as a migraine relief.

Stellaria media

Chickweed

Surely no gardener in his or her right mind would deliberately grow chickweed. Perhaps not, although, interestingly, the presence of a good natural growth of the plant is no bad thing; it indicates a soil rich in nitrogen. And who could fail to have a soft spot for a weed that can be eaten? Seen in isolation, it is really rather a charming little thing and a small patch in a large herb garden will cause no harm and give some rather useful and not least unexpectedly appetizing vegetation.

Above: *Common chickweed (*Stellaria media*).*
Right: *Chickweed is another tasty weed.*

Cultivation and Care

Grow as an annual, sowing the seed *in situ* and then allowing it to self-seed (try to stop it!), simply pulling out excess seedlings to keep the thing within bounds.

Chickweed Basics

Problems: None.

Recommended Varieties: The normal species is widely available; too widely available for many people's liking.

Ornamental Appeal: Rather dainty, creeping habit, small light green leaves and very tiny white flowers.

Site and Soil: Full sun to light shade and almost any soil but the richer and more moist (provided not waterlogged), the better it grows.

Hardiness: Very hardy, tolerating −20°C (−4°F).

Size: A single plant will produce a mass of growth of about 30 × 30cm (12 × 12in) within a season.

Chickweed Uses

Culinary Use the plant raw in salads (some gardeners eat it as they weed it from their vegetable patch). If you have sufficient, it may be lightly steamed and served as a vegetable; try it at your next dinner party and watch the faces when you tell them they're eating a common garden weed.

Non-Culinary Used to produce a wound-treating and inflammation-reducing poultice.

Symphytum officinale

Comfrey

Comfrey is one of those rarities: a plant that many gardeners grow with the specific intention of putting it on the compost heap. It has achieved almost divine status among the organic-growing fraternity for it is generally believed to contain more nutritional value as a fertilizer than any other type of plant. It may or may not have nutritional value, but while comfrey, an herbaceous perennial, certainly can be eaten, it should find a place in the herb garden for its medicinal value.

Cultivation and Care

Mulch in autumn and spring and give a balanced general fertilizer in spring. Cut down above-ground growth in autumn (or harvest leaves in bulk as needed; the plant will regenerate from the rootstock to the point of becoming invasive). Propagate by division in autumn.

Comfrey Basics

Problems: None.

Recommended Varieties: The normal *Symphytum officinale* is appropriate for the herb garden although other, slightly more attractive species are also available.

If your interest is in compost making, then the selected 'Bocking' strains are the ones to choose and are obtainable from specialist organic gardening suppliers.

Above: Comfrey is often used in the treatment of skin conditions.
Left: Comfrey (Symphytum officinale).

Ornamental Appeal:

Not very great; large, coarse bristly leaves on a large coarse plant with small, pendulous red and blue flowers. As with so many other species in the Boraginaceae family, the flowers seem too small for the plant.

Site and Soil: Full sun, in fairly rich and moist but not waterlogged soil.

Hardiness: Very hardy, tolerating −20°C (−4°F).

Size: Will attain 1– 1.5m × 60cm (3– 5ft × 24in) in two years.

Comfrey Uses

Culinary Young leaves may be used in salads or cooked as a vegetable but even when young, they are coarse and unappealing.

Non-Culinary A skin preparation is made from the leaves and used to treat rashes, eczema and other irritations.

Tagetes patula
French Marigold

Tagetes patula has a great deal to answer for. Firstly, it has introduced far too many gardeners to a multitude of F1 hybrid African, French and Afro-French marigolds that flood both the seed market and a great many gardens every summer. Secondly, the undoubted fact that its roots exude a secretion inhibitory to certain types of nematodes (eelworm) has also resulted in it being recommended as a cure-all for a vast range of quite unrelated garden pests and diseases. But there's no denying the wide interest in this plant, hence its inclusion.

Cultivation and Care

Grow as a half-hardy annual, sowing the plants in the greenhouse in spring for hardening-off and planting out when the danger of frost has passed.

French Marigold Basics

Problems: None.

Recommended Varieties: The small-flowered species are more charming than the large-flowered hybrids.

Ornamental Appeal: Pretty, finely divided, fern-like leaves and small, golden-yellow, double daisy flowers in summer.

Site and Soil: Full sun, in fairly rich and moist but free-draining soil.

Hardiness: Barely hardy, tolerating no less than −5°C (23°F).

Size: Will attain 25–30cm (10–12in) within the season.

Above: Tagetes patula – *Marigold (Triploid) Belles Series 'Mata Hari'.*
Left: Tagetes erecta *(French marigold).*

French Marigold Uses

Culinary None.

Non-Culinary No medicinal properties although a yellow dye is obtained from the flowers. The foliage, which has an acquired but pleasant fragrance, finds a place in potpourri.

Tanacetum balsamita

Alecost, Costmary

Even by the standards of the daisy family, the flowers of alecost are insignificant, rather like those of impoverished groundsel, but it is a plant well worth growing for its herbal value and for its long and interesting history. Attached to it is one of the most entertaining of herbal uses; it is said that Puritan settlers took the plant with them to North America because chewing its leaves was a useful way of passing the hours during long and tedious sermons. The odd name 'alecost' comes, incidentally, from another old use in flavouring ale, 'cost' meaning a spicy herb.

Cultivation and Care

Mulch in autumn and spring and give a balanced general fertilizer in spring. Cut down above-ground growth in autumn. Propagate this herbaceous perennial by sowing in pots in a soil-based compost in a cold-frame in late spring.

Alecost Basics

Problems: None

Recommended Varieties: The normal species is usually the only form available.

Ornamental Appeal: Almost none.

Site and Soil: Full sun, in light but moderately rich although well-drained soil.

Hardiness: Hardy to very hardy, tolerating −15 to −20°C (5 to −4°F).

Size: around 90 × 45cm (34 × 18in).

Alecost Uses

Culinary Young leaves may be chopped with cooked meats, in stuffings and soups to impart a slightly bitter flavour.

Non-Culinary An infusion is used for colds, the relief of stings and other minor ailments and also to aid childbirth.

Left: *Alecost, Costmary (*Tanacetum balsamita*).*
Right: *Cup of alecost tea.*

Tanacetum cinerariifolium

Pyrethrum

Superficially, pyrethrum looks like almost any other single daisy, with its yellow and white flowers and finely divided leaves. But its name is familiar because the flowers have for a long time been a source of a relatively safe insecticide (which is harmless to mammals) and it is for this important reason that it is included here; this herbaceous perennial has no direct non-culinary or culinary value. Although the extraction of the active principle isn't easy, the dried and crushed flowers themselves are a pretty reliable deterrent for crawling insects.

Right: *flowering Pyrethrum (*Tanacetum cinerariifolium*).*

Cultivation and Care

Mulch in autumn and spring and give a balanced general fertilizer in spring. Cut down above-ground growth in autumn. Propagate by division or by seed sown *in situ* in spring.

Pyrethrum Basics

Problems: None.

Recommended Varieties: The normal species only is available.

Ornamental Appeal: A typical single daisy with orange-centred, white-rayed flowers and finely divided, feathery leaves.

Site and Soil: Full sun, in light but moderately rich although well-drained soil.

Hardiness: Hardy to very hardy, tolerating −15 to −20°C (5 to −4°F).

Size: Around 80 × 40cm (32 × 16in) after two years.

Pyrethrum Uses

Culinary None.
Non-Culinary None.

Tanacetum parthenium

Feverfew

Chewing feverfew leaves provides welcome relief for many migraine sufferers. Its important herbal properties aside, it is a pretty plant – especially in its golden foliaged variant – producing many daisy-like flowers in white and orange. For propagation purposes, this herbaceous perennial is useful as it self-seeds slightly aggressively.

Cultivation and Care

Mulch in autumn and spring and give a balanced general fertilizer in spring. Cut down above-ground growth in autumn. Propagate by division or by seed sown *in situ* in spring.

Feverfew Basics

Problems: None.

Recommended Varieties: The normal species only is widely available but a prettier form is the golden-leafed 'Aureum' that comes true from seed. Double-flowered and pure white-flowered forms are also often seen under various names. Their leaves are equally effective as a migraine treatment.

Above and left: *Feverfew*
*(*Tanacetum parthenium*).*

Site and Soil: Full sun, in light but moderately rich although well-drained soil.

Hardiness: Hardy to very hardy, tolerating −15 to −20°C (5 to −4°F).

Size: Around 60 × 20cm (24 × 8in) after two years.

Feverfew Uses

Culinary Leaves may be used in salads and as flavourings although they are rather bitter.

Non-Culinary Use fresh leaves to reduce migraine incidence. The usual recommendation is for three or four fresh leaves daily in sandwiches as some people find the plant causes irritation to the lips if chewed alone.

Taraxacum officinale

Dandelion

Few things can match the sheer spectacle of a mass of dandelion flowers in early summer, even if they are growing on your lawn. A common feature of French cuisine, dandelion leaves make excellent eating, which is just one example of the herbal versatility of this much-maligned herbaceous perennial.

Cultivation and Care

The problem is in restricting it. The best plan is as with horseradish (see pages 68–9): sink a square-sided and bottomless container in the soil and grow the plants in it, then uproot and replant from small root pieces every spring. Remove seeds to restrict spread.

Dandelion Basics

Problems: None.

Recommended Varieties: Selected culinary strains are available.

Right: *Dandelions (*Taraxacum officinale*)*.
Opposite: *Salad of young dandelion leaves*.

Ornamental Appeal: Too well known to justify detailed description; bright golden-yellow flowers and deeply toothed leaves ('dent de lion').

Site and Soil: Full sun to very light shade; tolerant of most soils except very acidic or very alkaline sites.

Hardiness: Very hardy, tolerating −20°C (−4°F).

Size: Will attain from 10– 30 × 10– 20cm (4– 12 × 4– 8in) within a season, depending on the growing conditions.

Dandelion Uses

Culinary Young leaves are delicious in salads, and are even more tender if forced. Dried roots may also be ground to produce a substitute for coffee that is at least as good as chicory.

Non-Culinary A number of medicinal properties are claimed: a skin treatment is prepared from the leaves and a preparation made from the roots that, among others, gives relief from constipation and insomnia.

Thymus spp.

Thyme

Thymes must be at the same time among the best known but also the least appreciated and understood of common herbs. Far too many gardeners grow inappropriate species and varieties: ornamental ones where they need culinary forms, and creeping types when what they really want is a miniature bush. But whichever of the many forms you decide is correct for you, there can be no doubt that a herb garden, indeed a garden of any sort, without some thymes, is scarcely worthy of the name. They have been grown, written and sung about, praised and used since antiquity and will be a part of gardening for as long as people garden.

Left: *Thyme herbs (Thymus vulgaris).*
Right: *Fresh sprigs of thyme.*

Cultivation and Care

Little needed once fully established although best when lightly mulched in autumn and spring and given a little balanced general fertilizer in spring. Propagate by semi-ripe cuttings in late summer, rooted in a light, soil-based compost in a cold-frame. This is best done every second year and the stock plants replaced by the new plants in the following season. Shrubby perennials, thyme species may be raised from seed but unfortunately all that you will obtain are the generally straggly wild forms. The best varieties are always propagated by cuttings which are fairly easy to strike.

Thyme Basics

Problems: None.

Recommended Varieties: Approximately one hundred species or varieties of thyme are fairly widely obtainable and so here we shall concentrate on the most important herbal types. *Thymus* x *citriodorus* (lemon-scented thyme), untidy little shrub with pale pink flowers; the best forms are the coloured-leaf variants 'Golden Queen', with golden leaves, 'Silver Queen', more creeping than bushy with irregularly variegated leaves. Other common varieties such as 'Doone Valley', 'Archer's Gold' or 'Bertram Anderson' are for ornamental use.

T. herba-barona, slightly straggly, arching-creeping form with caraway flavour.

T. pulegioides (broad-leaved thyme), a native species with larger, broader leaves and a good typical thyme flavour.

T. pseudolanuginosus (woolly thyme), a creeping form with bright pink flowers and woolly leaves.

T. serpyllum 'Pink Chintz', grey-green leaves, and small, pink flowers in clusters.

T. vulgaris, the so-called wild thyme in its wild form is unkempt and straggly although it is strongly flavoured. The best form to choose is the neat, bush-like 'Silver Posie'. It has variegated leaves and is considered by many to be the best of all culinary varieties of thyme.

Ornamental Appeal: Evergreen leaves in shades of green, silver or gold. Small, pink flowers but white in some forms.

Above: *Flavouring fish with fresh thyme.*
Left: Thymus serpyllum *'Pink Chintz'.*

Site and Soil: Full sun, in light but moderately rich although well-drained soil; ideally neutral or slightly alkaline.

Hardiness: Hardy to very hardy, tolerating −15 to −20°C (5 to −4°F).

Size: Varies according to species from around 5 × 25cm (2 × 10in) for the smaller creeping forms to 45 × 25cm (18 × 10in) for the more vigorous bush varieties.

Thyme Uses

Culinary Chopped leaves and flowers can be added to almost any savoury dish you wish, but they are especially good in salads and stuffings and also with cooked meats. The sweeter-flavoured forms may be used in desserts.

Non-Culinary An infusion of the leaves is very refreshing and can give relief from sore throats and headaches.

Trigonella foenum-graecum

Fenugreek

Far more people these days eat fenugreek than know what it is, for its sprouted seeds turn up anonymously in oriental restaurants. It has been used for centuries in a wide variety of ways and, quite apart from its herbal properties, it is extensively grown, like other members of the bean and pea family, as a fodder crop. It has a wide natural

distribution in both southern Europe and Asia, which explains why it was important for peoples as distantly separated as the Greeks and the natives of southern India. As befits its origins, it is tender, but, being an annual, this is no bar to its cultivation in herb gardens.

Cultivation and Care

Grow as a half-hardy annual, sowing seed *in situ* in mid-spring in rows 20cm (8in) apart.

Fenugreek Basics
Problems: None.

Right: *Fenugreek seeds.*
Left: *Fenugreek (*Trigonella foenum-graecum*).*

Ornamental Appeal: Rather slight; trifoliate, clover-like leaves and small, yellowish pea-like flowers in summer.

Site and Soil: Full sun, in light, but moderately rich although well-drained and preferably alkaline soil.

Hardiness: Barely hardy, tolerating no less than −5°C (23°F).

Size: A scrambling habit to produce an untidy plant 60–75cm (24–30in) tall.

Fenugreek Uses

Culinary Sprouted seeds are used in and with oriental and other dishes. Larger plants cooked as a vegetable, in the manner of spinach. Roasted and ground seeds are a component of curries and other spices.

Non-Culinary The refreshing fragrances, either fresh or as infusions give relief from nasal congestion, headaches and other discomforts. Crushed seeds make an unappetizing drink, said to ease flatulence.

Tropaeolum majus

Nasturtium

Thanks to the enterprise of supermarkets in including nasturtium flowers among their summer salads, these bright orange blooms are often most people's introduction to blossom eating. They are far from being the only edible flowers but there are few that are more striking, easier to grow or that make such an imposing splash of colour in the garden as this annual.

Cultivation and Care
None needed once the seeds have been sown in spring and the seedlings fed until established.

Nasturtium Basics
Problems: Aphids and also large white butterfly caterpillars.

Recommended Varieties: Many varieties are sold for ornamental use and all forms are edible. Certainly the best for garden use are the climbing and scrambling varieties such as 'Tall Mixed' and 'Giant Climbing Mixed' (the nasturtium isn't blessed with the most imaginative names), but among others are dwarf, double-flowered and variegated forms.

Ornamental Appeal: Unique; large, usually single flowers in vivid orange, yellow, red and cream with large rounded, full green leaves on a vigorous scrambling plant.

Site and Soil: Full sun, in light and impoverished soil. In fertile conditions, flowers will be few and the leaves more abundant.

Hardiness: Barely hardy, tolerating no less than −5°C (23°F).

Size: The taller varieties produce a plant up to 3m (10ft) tall within the season.

Nasturtium Uses

Culinary Flowers and flower buds can be used in salads where they add a gentle tang to the flavour and, more importantly, a vivid colour contrast to the green of other ingredients. Young seed pods can also be eaten but are rather strongly flavoured and have little visual appeal.

Non-Culinary None.

Above: *Garden nasturtium (*Tropaeolum majus*) allowed to scramble along a fence.*
Left: *Salad with edible nasturtium flowers.*

Tussilago farfara
Coltsfoot

Named for the hoof-shape (colt's foot) of its leaves, this herbaceous perennial is native to Europe and Asia and common in North and South America. The bright yellow flowers, which have a superficial resemblance to those of the dandelion, appear in early spring.

Cultivation and Care

Almost none needed, but plant should be lifted and divided every two years for they will otherwise become highly invasive. Propagate by division, from root fragments or from seed sown in

pots in a soil-based compost in a cold-frame during late spring.

Coltsfoot Basics

Problems: None.

Recommended Varieties: Normal species only is available.

Ornamental Appeal: Unusually pretty although rather small, bright yellow flowers on bare, thick, scaly stems; large, more-or-less rounded leaves with woolly undersides emerge from the soil after the flowers.

Site and Soil: Full sun or light shade, in almost any soils, even those which are impoverished; also heavy sites provided they are fairly damp.

Hardiness: Very hardy, tolerating −20°C (−4°F).

Size: Will attain approximately 30 × 45cm (12 × 18in) within two years.

Above: *Herbal tea made with coltsfoot flowers.*
Left: *Coltsfoot (*Tussilago farfara*)*.

Coltsfoot Uses

Culinary Young leaves can be used in salads together with chopped flowers.

Non-Culinary An infusion is used for the relief of congestion and coughs.

Urtica dioica

Stinging Nettle

Not so long ago, anyone who deliberately grew stinging nettles would have been thought slightly peculiar. Then came the vogue for helping wildlife and the realization that the nettle is the food plant for some most attractive butterflies; and everyone wanted to grow a patch. The nettle was also much sought after in wartime, when ordinary beer was in short supply. In addition to most parts having been eaten at some time, the stems yield a strong fibre woven since the Bronze Age.

Cultivation and Care

Little needed once this herbaceous perennial is established although, as it can be invasive and is such a successful weed, it is best confined by vertical slabs in the soil; or alternatively, lifted and divided every autumn. Propagate by division or from seed sown *in situ* in spring.

Left: *Stinging nettle (*Urtica dioica*).*

Right: *Nettle soup is traditionally made from fresh spring leaves.*

Stinging Nettle Basics

Problems: None.

Recommended Varieties: Normal species only is available.

Ornamental Appeal: The plant is distinctly unremarkable although the greenish, catkin-like flowers have some appeal if you can forget that the overall bristly appearance is the result of masses of highly irritant stinging hairs (the effect of which, incidentally, is lost after cooking).

Site and Soil: Full sun to moderate shade; will tolerate most soils but best on rich, moist loams.

Hardiness: Very hardy, tolerating −20°C (−4°F).

Size: In good soil will attain over 1m × 30cm (3ft × 12in) within two years.

Stinging Nettle Uses

Culinary Young leaves and shoots may be cooked as a highly nutritious and moderately tasty vegetable, and the plant can also be used as the basis of nettle beer.

Non-Culinary An infusion of the young leaves produces a tonic with rather general 'health-giving' properties.

Valeriana officinalis
Valerian

This can be confused with *Centranthus*, the red valerian which has larger, more-or-less undivided leaves and little herbal value. *Valeriana*, however, has been used for centuries and in many parts of the world for a wide range of purposes, some related to its most unusual, not to say bizarre smell.

Left: Valeriana officinalis.
Right: *Dried valerian roots.*

Cultivation and Care

Mulch in autumn and spring and apply a balanced general fertilizer in spring. Cut down above-ground growth in autumn. Propagate this herbaceous perennial by division, although this must be performed carefully for the rootstock is easily damaged; from seed, sown in a soil-based compost in a cold-frame during spring is better.

Valerian Basics

Problems: Aphids.

Recommended Varieties: Normal species only is available.

Ornamental Appeal: Heads of small, pale pink flowers on tall stems with divided leaves; pretty but not distinguished.

Site and Soil: Full sun to moderate shade; tolerates most soils but best on fairly rich, organic sites.

Hardiness: Very hardy, tolerating −20°C (−4°F).

Size: Will attain approximately 1–1.5m × 50cm (3–5ft × 20in) in two or three years.

Valerian Uses

Culinary Roots may be cooked as a vegetable or used to add flavour (albeit a rather odd one) to cooked meat dishes, soups and stews.

Non-Culinary Root extracts have been used to make a preparation that is alleged to cure everything from insomnia to exhaustion but as the same substance is also recommended to attract cats, rats and earthworms, you may be reluctant to give it a personal trial.

Verbascum thapsus
Mullein

Mullein plants are unmistakable and it is a great shame that, as biennials, those tall, closely packed spikes of yellow and orange flowers (and perhaps less attractive to some eyes, the pink, as in some of the cultivated forms) last only two years. But they aren't plants that you can ignore and they make remarkable ornamental subjects as well as having ancient herbal value.

Cultivation and Care
Grow as a biennial, sowing seed in pots of soil-based compost in a cold-frame in spring and then plant out into flowering positions later in the summer.

Mullein Basics

Problems: Mildew.

Recommended Varieties: The normal species only is available of *Verbascum thapsus*. Cultivated ornamental species may lack herbal properties and be significantly toxic.

Ornamental Appeal: Tall, striking flower spikes that emerge from a large rosette of distinctly woolly leaves.

Site and Soil: Full sun, in light, free-draining but not very rich, alkaline soil.

Hardiness: Very hardy, tolerating −20°C (−4°F)

Size: Attains 2m × 50cm (7ft × 20in) within the two seasons.

Mullein Uses

Culinary None.

Non-Culinary Leaves and/or flowers are used to produce remedies for migraine and respiratory problems but must be used with care and preferably under supervision because of the possible toxicity.

Left: *Mullein (*Verbascum thapsus*).*
Right: *Dried mullein flowers.*

Verbena officinalis

Vervain

Vervain is truly one of the most unappealing and insignificant of plants and yet it has a herbal history as long and distinguished as that of any herb. Egyptians, Greeks, Romans, Persians, and even humble Anglo-Saxons had a special place for it in their medicine and mythology. It can't really be excluded from any comprehensive herb collection and yet, ideally, it should be tucked away inconspicuously.

Cultivation and Care

Mulch lightly in the autumn and spring and give a balanced general fertilizer in the spring. Cut down above-ground growth in the late autumn. Propagation for this herbaceous perennial is by division or alternatively from seed sown *in situ* in the spring.

Vervain Basics

Problems: None.

Recommended Varieties: Normal species only is available.

Right: *Vervain (*Verbena officinalis*).*
Opposite: *Dried vervain is used as a herbal remedy.*

Ornamental Appeal: Almost non-existent; faintly chrysanthemum-like leaves and minute mauve flowers on rather spindly spikes.

Site and Soil: Prefers full sun to light shade; will tolerate most soils but tends to do best on loams that are rich, moist and organic.

Hardiness: Very hardy, will tolerate up to −20°C (−4°F).

Size: Will attain 75cm–1m × 30cm (30in–3ft × 12in) within three years.

Vervain Uses

Culinary None.

Non-Culinary An infusion is used to treat sore throats, as a general sedative and, paradoxically, as an aphrodisiac.

Vinca major

Periwinkle

The periwinkles are among the most useful and valuable evergreen ground-cover plants and are especially useful in that most difficult of environments, dry shade. It comes as a surprise, albeit a pleasing one, however, to discover that they have some herbal value, too. They make ideal plants, therefore, for difficult areas in a large herb garden and, although in a more confined space, the lesser species *Vinca minor* would be most appropriate, it is the more robust *Vinca major* that has the better herbal pedigree.

Cultivation and Care

Ideally, should be mulched in autumn and spring although this is difficult once established as ground cover. Give a balanced general fertilizer in spring. Cut down above-ground growth in spring to encourage fresh new shoots. Propagate this shrubby/herbaceous perennial by division, by removal of natural layers from autumn to spring, or by semi-ripe cuttings in a soil-based compost in a cold-frame during summer.

Periwinkle Basics

Problems: Rust.

Left: *Greater periwinkle (*Vinca major*).*

Recommended Varieties: There are many different varieties of *Vinca major* with various flower colours and leaf variegations, but rather fewer of *V. major* although 'Variegata' is an attractively variegated and rather less aggressive form while *alba* is white flowered.

Ornamental Appeal: Glossy, broadly elongated, evergreen leaves carried on arching, ground-covering stems with bright blue flowers.

Site and Soil: Full sun to moderate shade; tolerates almost all soils including dry conditions.

Above: Vinca major 'Variegata'.

Hardiness: Very hardy, tolerating −20°C (−4°F).

Size: Will attain 50cm × 1m (20in × 3ft) within three years.

Periwinkle Uses

Culinary None.

Non-Culinary A treatment for diabetes is prepared from the leaves although various supposedly wound-healing poultices were also once made from the plant.

Viola odorata

Sweet Violet

Irish gardener and writer William Robinson, who had a refreshingly simple approach, advised using violets as a living mulch under shrub roses. Sweet violet will spread fairly effectively without any intervention, be it planted in a rose garden or a herb garden. The sweet violet, with its attractively perfumed, purple flowers, is as old as gardening and there is scarcely a classical writer or poet who hasn't made some allusion to its beauty and its many properties.

Cultivation and Care

Almost none is needed once this perennial is established but a balanced general fertilizer should be given in spring. Propagate by division or by removal of naturally rooted runners.

Sweet Violet Basics

Problems: None.

Recommended Varieties: The normal species is the one that you will usually find although there are, as usual, double and white-flowered variants and a small group of the latter does look very pretty when inter-planted with the wild form.

Ornamental Appeal: A typical violet with its small, purple flowers arising from a trailing, ground-covering rootstock; it is especially welcome for appearing in the cold early months of the year.

Site and Soil: Prefers light to moderate shade; tolerates most soils, including dry sites, but best in rich, moist loams.

Hardiness: Very hardy, tolerating −20°C(−4°F).

Size: Will attain 15 × 30cm (6 × 12in) within three years.

Left: *Sweet violet (*Viola odorata*).*
Above: *Candied violets.*

Sweet Violet Uses

Culinary Crystallized violets have long been used as cake decorations and a rather sickly sweet syrup may also be made from them.

Non-Culinary Infusions may be prepared from flowers, leaves and roots, and are beneficial in many medicinal applications, especially the relief of head colds and congestion.

HERBAL TREES AND SHRUBS

Several of the plants described in the book are either more-or-less shrubby or are undeniably genuine shrubs. But there are also a number of ornamental shrubs and trees that have interesting or valuable herbal properties. You might like to consider their inclusion in a comprehensive herb collection or put them to use as a hedge or as a shelter belt for the protection of more tender specimens.

Buxus sempervirens

Box

Box is a part of folklore, a plant that has been appreciated for centuries for its beautiful, hard, close-grained wood. Its role in the formal herb garden is an invaluable one, however, for in its slow-growing form, it is without peer as an edging and is seen at its best in the ultimate formality of knot gardens. Its growth rate, dense habit and evergreen leaves make this shrub indispensable.

Above: *Clipped box shrub in ornamental pot.*

Left: Buxus sempervirens 'Suffruticosa' hedge.

Box Uses
Culinary None.
Non-Culinary None.

Cultivation and Care
Mulch in autumn and give a balanced general fertilizer in spring. Clip twice each year, ideally in mid-summer and mid-autumn. Propagate by semi-ripe cuttings in a soil-based compost in a cold-frame during summer or by hardwood cuttings in autumn.

Box Basics
Problems: Whitefly, box sucker, box blight and aphids.

Recommended Varieties: The normal species is widely obtainable and easily the least expensive form. 'Suffruticosa' is the slow-growing form to use for edging. Although often assumed inherently dwarf, it will, if unpruned, become rather a tall shrub. To add variety to a planting of 'Suffruticosa', specimens of one of the variegated types may be dotted among it: either 'Argenteovariegata', with white-margined leaves, or 'Aureovariegata' with golden leaf edges and some small blotches.

Functional Value: As dwarf edging or as a specimen ornamental.

Ornamental Appeal: Small, rounded, evergreen leaves, some with variegation; yellowish flowers.

Site and Soil: Full sun to moderate or almost deep shade; tolerates most soils but best on rich, moist and preferably alkaline loams.

Hardiness: Very hardy, tolerating −20°C (−4°F).

Size: The more vigorous types will attain 5–6 × 5–6m (16–20 × 16–20ft) but are usually clipped to much less.

Eucalyptus spp.

Gum tree

Many species of eucalyptus are undeniably possessed of beautiful foliage and a distinctive aroma. When mature, either as individual specimens or as extensive forests, they present an imposing sight, but other than as isolated trees they are perhaps best left in their native forests in Australia as they have a tendency to be invasive and competitive. But a small, well-contained plant of the hardy *Eucalyptus globulus* should find a ready welcome in the herb garden.

Cultivation and Care

Mulch in autumn and spring and give a balanced fertilizer in spring. Prune back to within 30cm (12in) of soil level in spring to encourage a dwarf, shrubby habit with the attractive juvenile foliage. Allowed to grow tall, the tree will soon become less

attractive, out of hand and more prone to damage from frost and wind. Propagated most readily from seed sown in a soil-based compost in a cold-frame during late spring.

Eucalyptus Basics

Problems: Scale insects and sooty mould growth.

Recommended Varieties: *Eucalyptus* is a huge genus of nearly 500 species, most too tender to be grown outdoors in colder climates. The hardiest species for the herb garden is the blue gum, *E. globulus*.

Functional Value: As a specimen ornamental, if given some shelter.

Ornamental Appeal: Rounded, glaucous young foliage; elongated, spearhead-shaped mature leaves; peeling, grey bark.

Site and Soil: Full sun with shelter from cold winds; tolerates most soils but best on rich, organic loams.

Hardiness: Fairly hardy, tolerating around −10°C (14°F).

Size: Allowed to reach maturity in mild areas, *E. globulus* will attain 15m (50ft) after ten years and ultimately perhaps 40m (120ft).

Left: *Tasmanian blue gum (*Eucalyptus globulus*).
Below: *Eucalyptus oil.*

Gum Tree Uses

Culinary None.

Non-Culinary Leaves provide oil used in cough and cold remedies and also as a treatment for burns and other skin complaints.

Gaultheria procumbens

Wintergreen

The various species of *Gaultheria* are among a group of sound, workhorse shrubs for the ornamental garden. They are pretty enough and functional enough but they will never be stars of any border. And yet oil of wintergreen, together with witch hazel (see page 290) must be among the most familiar, and probably most effective of herbal medicines still in everyday use.

Cultivation and Care

Mulch in autumn and spring and give a balanced general fertilizer in spring. No pruning is needed but it may be cut back hard in spring and it will regenerate. Most easily propagated by removal of suckers.

Left: *Wintergreen (*Gaultheria procumbens*).* **Right:** Gaultheria procumbens *fruits*.

Wintergreen Basics

Problems: None.

Recommended Varieties: Normal species only is available.

Functional Value: As evergreen ground cover.

Ornamental Appeal: Small, more or less oval, glossy, dark green, evergreen leaves, bunches of drooping, white, summer flowers and bright red, autumn berries.

Site and Soil: Light to moderate shade in most soils, preferably acidic; intolerant of alkalinity.

Hardiness: Moderately hardy to hardy, tolerating around −15°C (5°F).

Size: Will attain about 50 × 75cm (20 × 30in) after three years and about 50cm × 3m (20in × 10ft) eventually.

Wintergreen Uses

Culinary A strange tasting 'tea' can be made from the leaves.

Non-Culinary An oil from the leaves has healing and pain-relieving properties and is applied to inflamed skin. An infusion is taken as a relief for sore throats.

Hamamelis virginiana

Witch Hazel

Witch hazel and wintergreen (see page 288) are familiar names to people who haven't the remotest idea what either of the plants look like. You can walk into any pharmacy and find bottles so labelled on the shelf, as both plants produce widely used and effective soothing remedies. Witch hazel is much more appealing of the two and is worthy of a place in any garden for its winter flowers. But it is not any easy shrub, requiring exacting conditions if it is to grow well.

Cultivation and Care

Mulch in autumn and spring and give a balanced general or rose fertilizer in spring. Do not prune. Propagation is difficult from cuttings but the true species may be raised from seed sown in pots of soil-based compost in a cold-frame; germination is slow.

Left: *Witch hazel (*Hamamelis virginiana*).* **Right:** *Witch hazel cream.*

Witch Hazel Basics

Problems: None.

Recommended Varieties: The best-known ornamental witch hazels are the Asiatic species, most notably *Hamamelis mollis*, but the best for the extraction of medicinal witch hazel is the North American *H. virginiana*, which provides the rootstock onto which the ornamental forms are grafted.

Functional Value: None.

Ornamental Appeal: Small fragrant, yellow flowers borne on twigs in late autumn, coincident with the foliage turning yellow before dropping. The impact, therefore, is not as great as that of the Asiatic species which flower later in the winter on bare twigs.

Site and Soil: Light shade and shelter from cold winds, in moist, free-draining organic soil, ideally slightly acidic.

Hardiness: Moderately hardy, tolerating about −15°C (5°F) but damaged by cold winds.

Size: Will attain 1 × 1m (3 × 3ft) after three years and up to 5–6 × 5m (15–20 × 15ft) eventually.

Witch Hazel Uses

Culinary None.

Non-Culinary An extract from the young shoots is used for the relief of bruises, inflammations and other external sores.

Ilex aquifolium

Holly

It is a curious phenomenon that everyone seems to forget about the holly plant after the festive season and then bring it to mind again for Christmas. However, there is far more to this shrub than a bunch of prickly leaves and some red berries for decoration. The holly genus, *Ilex*, includes a very wide range of evergreen as well as many deciduous species, most without significant prickles and not all with red berries. Like box, it has long been grown for its extremely hard wood, which can be worked into most attractive ornamental items, but it also has unexpected and ancient herbal properties, too.

Cultivation and Care

Mulch in autumn and spring and give a balanced general fertilizer in spring. The hedgehog hollies need no pruning; but others may be clipped as required in mid-summer and mid-autumn. They are all but impossible to strike from cuttings and the named forms do not come true from their seed.

Holly Basics

Problems: Leaf miners (which are disfiguring but not damaging).

Recommended Varieties: Although there are many ornamental varieties of holly, derived from several

Above: *Branch of holly with red berries.*
Left: *English holly (*Ilex aquifolium *'Golden King').*

species, it is the common holly, *Ilex aquifolium*, that has been used for herbal purposes. The best forms for the herb garden are the varieties of the dwarf, so-called hedgehog holly, 'Ferox'. 'Ferox Argentea' has silver leaf edges and 'Ferox Aurea' an irregular golden variegation. For a taller tree, choose 'J.C. Van Tol' or 'Golden Queen'.

Functional Value: As either hedging or a specimen ornamental.

Ornamental Appeal: Evergreen leaves, red or yellow berries and an attractive, dense, if sometimes impenetrable habit.

Site and Soil: Full sun to moderate shade; tolerates most soils provided they are not extremely wet or extremely dry.

Hardiness: Very hardy, tolerating −20°C (−4°F).

Size: Hedgehog holly will attain about 75 × 75cm (30 × 30in) after four or five years and perhaps 2 × 2m (7 × 7ft) eventually. Other varieties will attain about 1m × 50cm (3ft × 20in) after three or four years and ultimately form trees of about 10–15m (30–50ft) in height.

Holly Uses

Culinary None.

Non-Culinary An infusion from the leaves is used to relieve congestion and colds.

Laurus nobilis

Sweet Bay

This is perhaps the most valuable of all shrubby herbs, although it is amazing the number of people who grow it as an ornamental, generally in the form of over-priced specimens in terracotta pots, and yet still buy bay leaves from their supermarket. The number of leaves that are required in the kitchen would not make much impression on so robust a plant.

Cultivation and Care

Mulch in autumn and spring and give a balanced general fertilizer in spring. These shrubs/trees may be clipped to shape in summer and will also regenerate from the old wood if cut back hard. Propagate from semi-ripe cuttings in a soil-based compost in a cold-frame during the summer.

Sweet Bay Basics

Problems: Scale insects, leading to the development of sooty moulds.

Left: *Sweet bay (*Laurus nobilis*).*
Right: *Bay leaves bouquet.*

Recommended Varieties: The normal species is the one to choose although there is a rather more tender form, 'Aurea', supposedly golden-leaved but to some eyes merely resembling a sick version of the normal one.

Functional Value: As an attractive specimen ornamental, most effective when clipped to shape.

Ornamental Appeal: Elongated, dull green, evergreen leaves and green-yellow flowers in early summer.

Site and Soil: Full sun to moderate shade with shelter from cold winds. Tolerates most soils provided they are not very wet, heavy and cold.

Hardiness: Moderately hardy, tolerating −10 to −15°C (14 to 5°F) but damaged by cold winds.

Size: Will attain about 1.5 × 1.5m (5 × 5ft) after four or five years and, unpruned, could eventually form a tree of about 12 × 9m (40 × 28ft).

Sweet Bay Uses

Culinary Leaves are used with cooked meat of all types, also with some fish and in soups and stews. Most commonly used in *bouquets garnis*. Older leaves are the best.

Non-Culinary A leaf infusion is used as a refreshing stimulant to the appetite.

Morus nigra

Black Mulberry

The mulberry is a native of south-western Asia that is grown widely around the world. As a herb plant, the mulberry crosses the boundary into being one of those plants that is grown for an edible product rather than a flavouring. But it is used for medicinal as well as straightforward edible purposes and it is such a splendid tree, both stately and long-lived, that it deserves a place here.

Cultivation and Care

Mulch in autumn and spring and give a balanced general fertilizer in spring. No pruning is necessary. Propagate by seed sown fresh into an acidic, soilless compost or by semi-hardwood cuttings in a soil-based compost in a cold-frame during summer.

Black Mulberry Basics

Problems: None.

Recommended Varieties: The normal species is widely available although one or two named forms are also sometimes offered. The white mulberry *Morus alba*, is a similar species to the black, but it has rather tasteless fruit. This is the species whose leaves are used for feeding silkworms and thus contribute to the making of silk.

Functional Value: None.

Ornamental Appeal: Deciduous and rather dull when with its greenish catkins but most attractive when covered with the dark red, raspberry-like fruit – which are notorious for dropping off the tree and staining clothing.

Site and Soil: Full sun in sheltered sites, on rich, moist but well-drained loams.

Hardiness: Very hardy, tolerating −20°C (−4°F).

Size: Will attain about 2 × 1m (7 × 3ft) after three or four years and become a tree up to 12m (40ft) tall eventually.

Above: *A delicious bowl of mulberries.*
Left: *Black mulberry (*Morus nigra*).*

Black Mulberry Uses

Culinary Fruit eaten fresh is delicious but also good in fruit pies, jams or made into wine.

Non-Culinary Fruit is used to make a laxative syrup and a leaf infusion can be used by diabetics.

Myrica gale
Bog Myrtle

There aren't many garden shrubs that can really be called bog plants. Likewise, there aren't many herbs that thrive in really wet conditions. All of these attributes come together in this rather attractive plant. Not all herb gardens will have a suitable place for it, but a bog garden nearby would be very appropriate.

Above: *Bog myrtle or sweet gale (Myrica gale) catkins.*
Right: *Bog myrtle.*

Cultivation and Care

Mulch in autumn and spring and give a balanced general fertilizer in spring, at least until well established. No pruning is needed other than the cutting out of damaged branches on old trees. It may be propagated by means of the layering method if low branches are available or by hardwood cuttings in late autumn.

Bog Myrtle Basics

Problems: Fungal leaf spots and canker.

Recommended Varieties: Normal species only is available.

Functional Value: As a bog garden ornamental.

Ornamental Appeal: Deciduous with narrowly elongated, slightly toothed and woolly leaves, brown catkins and small, greenish-yellow flowers in spring.

Site and Soil: Light to moderate shade, in wet, cool, acidic and also preferably organic soils.

Hardiness: Very hardy, tolerating −20°C (−4°F).

Size: Will attain about 1 × 1m (3 × 3ft) after three or four years and up to about 2 × 2m (7 × 7ft) eventually.

Bog Myrtle Uses

Culinary Leaves, after drying, are used with cooked meats, in soups and stews and also to flavour alcoholic drinks.

Non-Culinary An infusion from the leaves is used to relieve gastric complaints.

Populus balsamifera

Balsam Poplar

There's no denying that the balsam poplar is a really big tree and not one likely to be planted solely for its herbal appeal. Indeed, its suckering habit can create problems but the fact remains that many gardens do contain specimens planted in the past and its herbal properties are interesting enough to justify its inclusion here. The buds of the potentially giant tree are covered with a yellow gum, but it is the unfolding white leaves which give off the distinctive smell of balsam.

Cultivation and Care
None needed once established but damaged branches should not be cut out regularly. Propagate by hardwood cuttings in autumn.

Balsam Poplar Basics
Problems: Canker, leaf curl, leaf rust, virus.

Recommended Varieties: Normal species only is available.

Functional Value: As a screening or shelter-belt tree.

Ornamental Appeal: Deciduous with large, more-or-less heart-shaped, dark

Left: *Balsam poplar (*Populus balsamifera*).*
Below: *The oil from balsam leaf buds are used to make Balm of Gilead.*

green leaves with whitish undersides and yellowish, pendent catkins in spring.

Site and Soil: Full sun, tolerates most soils provided deep, rich and moist.

Hardiness: Very hardy, tolerating −20°C (−4°F).

Size: A very vigorous plant which will attain about 2.5 × 1m (8 × 3ft) after two or three years and eventually become a tree up to 30m (100ft) tall.

Balsam Poplar Uses

Culinary None.

Non-Culinary A fragrant oil occurs in, of all places, the leaf buds which are highly sticky and give the entire plant a characteristic aroma. When extracted, it is used for many medicinal purposes including cough remedies, lung, gastric and renal complaints, and as the basis of an antiseptic and healing ointment.

Prunus dulcis

Almond

Almonds can't be grown in many temperate gardens as they are rather too tender; and in most areas, they suffer frightfully from leaf curl disease. But in places where it does thrive, the almond is a most charming tree and an ideal specimen to plant close to a herb garden. The combination of spring blossom and then a crop of nuts that offer a wide range of kitchen and herbal applications is unmatched by any other tree.

Cultivation and Care

Mulch in autumn and spring and give a balanced general fertilizer in the spring, at least until well established. No pruning is needed other than the cutting out of damaged branches on old trees, which must be done in spring or early summer to avoid the danger of infection by the fungus-causing silver leaf disease. Almonds can be propagated from seed and will generally produce worthwhile plants. Commercially, they are always grafted or budded.

Almond Basics

Problems: Peach leaf curl, silver leaf, aphids, brown rot.

Recommended Varieties: Many selected varieties are fine blossom trees but of little value for almond nut production, for which you need one of the selected culinary forms but, even so, it's important to be selective for the

varieties fall into two groups. Sweet almonds, generally with pink blossom, produce sweet edible nuts; bitter almonds, generally with white blossom, produce bitter nuts with poisonous kernels used for medicinal purposes.

Functional Value: None.

Ornamental Appeal: Deciduous, with elongated pointed and toothed leaves with some autumn colour. Very pretty pink or white spring blossom.

Site and Soil: Full sun in very sheltered and dry positions, on rich, moist but well-drained and preferably alkaline loams. In damp areas or situations, peach leaf curl disease will make almond growing impossible.

Hardiness: Moderately hardy, tolerating about −10 to −15°C (14 to 5°F) but blossom will be damaged by late frosts.

Size: Will attain about 3 × 1m (10 × 3ft) after three or four years and eventually become a tree up to 8–9m (25–28ft) tall.

Above: *Almond oil.*
Left: *Young almond fruits on* Prunus dulcis.

Almond Uses

Culinary Nuts are used in confectionery and also with cooked fish and other savoury dishes.

Non-Culinary Oil extracted from nuts is used as the basis of skin soothing and healing preparations and for minor medicinal applications.

Quercus spp.

Oak

No-one will consider planting an oak tree simply because of its herbal value; indeed it is unwise to plant oak trees in most gardens because of their potential ultimate size. But the fact remains that many large and older gardens already contain oaks, which may be protected by tree preservation legislation, and yet relatively few of their owners appreciate their herbal importance.

Cultivation and Care

Mulch in autumn and spring and give a balanced general fertilizer in spring. No pruning is needed other than the cutting out of damaged branches on old trees. Propagation from acorns, although selected forms are unlikely to come true and must be grafted; very difficult from cuttings.

Oak Basics

Problems: Mildew, many minor leaf and branch-attacking fungi and insects, which often cause concern but do no harm.

Recommended Varieties: There are two native oaks, *Quercus robur*, the pedunculate oak and *Q. petraea*, the sessile oak. Most existing garden trees will be of one of these species but for anyone who has space, one of the ornamental forms would be a wise

choice: *Q. robur* 'Concordia', golden leaves; *fastigata*, erect habit and 'Filicifolia', deeply divided leaves.

Functional Value: Provides shade and shelter.

Left and above: *Oak acorns.*

Ornamental Appeal: Deciduous, with indented leaves, greenish flowers in spring on mature trees, followed by acorns. Fairly good, if brief, autumn colour in some years.

Site and Soil: Full sun or light shade; tolerates most soils but best on rich, deep, well-drained loams.

Hardiness: Very hardy, tolerating −20°C (−4°F).

Size: 2 × 1m (7 × 3ft) after three or four years and eventually reaches up to 25m (8oft).

Oak Uses

Culinary Acorns can be roasted and ground to produce a coffee-like drink that was much used during the Second World War when real coffee was unobtainable.

Non-Culinary Bark extracts are used to prepare various medicinal treatments, principally for blood-related problems.

Rosa spp.

Rose

The rose is no longer quite the dominant force that once it was in gardens, but it remains an extremely popular flower in most parts of the world. Most gardens contain at least one rose and yet there cannot be many people who grow these important ornamental shrubs solely for their herbal value. There are, however, many culinary and non-culinary uses for the rose.

Cultivation and Care

Mulch in autumn and spring and give a balanced rose fertilizer in spring. The varieties recommended require little pruning other than the cutting out of damaged or congested shoots in spring and the removal of one or two of the oldest shoots each year. May be propagated from hardwood cuttings placed in a sheltered position in the garden in late autumn.

Rose Basics

Problems: Mildew, black spot, rust, aphids.

Recommended Varieties: For herbal purposes, these are invaluable: *Rosa* x *alba* ('White Rose of York'), single, white; *R. canina* (dog rose), single white or pink; *R.* x *centifolia* (Provence rose), double pink; *R.* x *damascena*

Right: *Sweet briar rose (*Rosa eglanteria*).*
Opposite: *Jar of rose petal jam.*

'Quatre Saisons', double, loose, pink; *R. eglanteria* (sweet briar), single, pink; *R. gallica*, single, rich pink and 'Rosa Mundi', pink and white striped.

Functional Value: As an ornamental sheltering screen.

Ornamental Appeal: It's worth remembering that some varieties will flower once only, some twice and some repeatedly; some have beautiful (and useful) hips; some have attractive autumn colours; and, in sheltered positions, most are more or less evergreen.

Site and Soil: Full sun, ideally in a sheltered spot. Tolerate most soils except very dry ones but they always do best in fairly heavy, moisture-retentive loams.

Hardiness: Hardy to very hardy, tolerating – 15° C to – 20°C (5°F to – 4°F).

Size: Varies with variety but most of those listed will attain about 1.2 × 1.5m (4 x 5ft) after three or four years.

Rose Uses

Culinary Petals (especially of the fragrant varieties) are used in confectionery, crystallized as a garnish or to make refreshing rose water. Hips (fruit) to produce jams, syrup, wine or herbal tea, rich in vitamin C.

Non-Culinary Infusion of leaves as a general 'healthy' tonic.

Rubus fruticosus

Bramble

Call it a bramble and most gardeners will spend considerable time, effort and money in trying to be rid of it. But call it a blackberry and they will carefully train and nurture it for the pleasure of picking fresh and succulent fruits in the autumn. In reality, although the best-flavoured fruits do come from wild plants, it is such a variable species that quality cannot be guaranteed and while one plant may yield a crop both delicious and bounteous, another will bear only a few shrivelled and tasteless berries. So while there is herbal value in the leaves, it makes sense to choose a selected, cultivated, fruiting variety.

Cultivation and Care

Mulch these shrubs in autumn and spring and give a balanced general fertilizer in spring. Cut out old fruited stems after the crop has been picked and tie in new shoots to training wires. Do not attempt to propagate from existing plants but buy new, virus-free stock.

Bramble Basics

Problems: Raspberry beetle, botrytis, rust, fungal leaf and cane spots.

Recommended Varieties: Given that you should select a cultivated form, it is important to choose one that is not too vigorous and can readily be contained in an average-sized garden. Among several candidates, particularly commended are 'Ashton Cross' and the thornless 'Loch Ness'.

Right: *Smoothie made with fresh blackberries.*
Left: *Blackberries (Rubus fruticosus).*

Functional Value:

When trained against a trellis or horizontal wires, may be used to form a boundary and wind-break.

Ornamental Appeal:
Deciduous (although more-or-less evergreen in many areas) with single white or pink flowers in spring followed by familiar fruits in late summer. Some varieties are thornless.

Site and Soil:
Full sun or light shade; tolerates most soils but will always crop best on rich, deep, well-drained loams, and in very dry or wet situations, will produce small, tasteless fruit.

Hardiness:
Very hardy, tolerating −20°C (−4°F).

Size:
Varies with variety, but with correct pruning, a single plant should attain a height and spread of about 2m (7ft) within two years.

Bramble Uses

Culinary In addition to the obvious uses of blackberries, fresh, cooked and preserved, remember their high vitamin C content.

Non-Culinary A leaf extract is used in preparations for general skin care and also in gargles and breath fresheners.

Taxus baccata

Yew

This is a most poisonous tree, the only non-toxic part being the red fleshy covering to the seed. But, like many another poisonous species, it does have herbal interest and as yew is also without peer as a hedging plant, there is no better boundary subject.

Left: *Yew (*Taxus baccata*).* **Right:** *Bright red berry-like covering of the yew's seeds.*

Cultivation and Care

Mulch in autumn and spring and give a general fertilizer in spring. Clip as necessary; hedges are best cut twice a year, once around mid-summer and once in mid-autumn. Propagate from seed sown in a soil-based compost in a cold-frame or from hardwood cuttings struck in a cold-frame in winter.

Yew Basics

Problems: None.

Recommended Varieties: For hedging, the normal species is the best plant, but for isolated specimens, choose 'Fastigiata Aurea' or 'Standishii' (both with golden foliage and columnar).

Functional Value: As a superb boundary hedge.

Ornamental Appeal: Rich, dark green foliage (or golden in selected forms), which contrasts with bright red fruits, although these will not develop on closely clipped hedges.

Site and Soil: Full sun to moderate shade; tolerates most soils but never successful on very dry sites.

Hardiness: Very hardy, tolerating −20°C (−4°F).

Size: When carefully clipped, forms a hedge of 2m × 45cm (7ft × 18in) within ten years. The golden-foliaged forms grow more slowly than this.

Yew Uses

Culinary None.

Non-Culinary Various medicinal herbal remedies are prepared from foliage and fruits.

Vitex agnus-castus
Monk's Pepper

A plant called monk's pepper certainly sounds like a herb and yet this is one of the least familiar of all herb plants and one of the least familiar garden trees. It has pretty, late summer flowers and beautifully fragrant foliage and, although it is relatively tender, it has many virtues and is worth giving a try in your herb garden.

Cultivation and Care
Mulch in the autumn and the spring and give a balanced general or rose fertilizer in the spring. Do not prune. Propagate from seed sown fresh in a soil-based compost in a cold-frame or from semi-ripe cuttings in a cold-frame in the summer.

Monk's Pepper Basics
Problems: None.

Recommended Varieties: The normal species will be the one most likely to be seen, although there is a selected flower colour form which is called 'Blue Spire'.

Functional Value: None.

Ornamental Appeal: Deciduous, with large, divided fragrant leaves and slender spikes of pale blue flowers in late summer; rather reminiscent of those of *Perovskia*.

Site and Soil: Full sun with shelter from cold winds; ideally close to a warm wall on light, free-draining soil; soils based on acidic sandstones are excellent.

Hardiness: Moderately hardy, tolerating −10°C (14°F).

Size: Will attain about 1.5 × 1m (5 × 3ft) after four or five years and about 4– 5m × 2m (13– 15 × 7ft) eventually.

Above: *Seeds of Monk's pepper are used in herbal remedies.*
Left: *Monk's pepper (*Vitex agnus-castus*).*

Monk's Pepper Uses

Culinary Ground seeds used as a spicy pepper substitute (and are supposedly aphrodisiac too).

Non-Culinary A medicinal treatment for menopausal problems is produced from the fruits.

Index

Acknowledgments

Picture Credits

Alamy Adelheid Nothegger/imageBROKER 74; Adrian Thomas/Science Photo Library 84; Angela Jordan 95; Anne Gilbert 202; Bildagentur-online 39, 43, 149, 169, 197, 257; bildagentur-online.com/th-foto 41, 129; blickwinkel/ Hecker 170; blickwinkel/Koenig 221; blickwinkel/Schmidbauer 206; Creativ Studio Heinemann/imageBROKER 289; D.Harms/WILDLIFE/Juniors Bildarchiv GmbH 37; Dieter Heinemann/Westend61 GmbH 139; Emilio Ereza 256; Florapix 226; Foodcollection.com 71; F. Strauss/Bon Appetit 87; Geoffrey Kidd 101, 119, 151, 279; geogphotos 244; Graham Uney 299; H. Reinhard/Arco Images GmbH 300; Hans-Joachim Schneider 177; Helen Guest 294; Holmes Garden Photos 138, 312; John Glover 114, 141, 152, 280, 288; Kathy Hancock 128; L. Ellert/Bon Appetit 79; MBP-Plants 6; MediaforMedical/Jean-Paul Chassenet 203; MNS Photo 231; Nature Photographers Ltd. 184; Nigel Cattlin 28, 29 below; O. Diez/Arco Images GmbH 103; Organica 281; Ottmar Diez/Bon Appetit 155; Paroli Galperti/CuboImages srl 217; Paroli Galperti/CuboImages srl 286; Pl-photo/isifa Image Service s.r.o. 232; Richard Clarkson 245; RM Floral 168; Science Photo Library 173; Steffen Hauser/botanikfoto 64, 220, 242, 246; tbkmedia. de 298; TH-Foto/doc-stock 109, 225; WILDLIFE GmbH 121, 171, 258; yogesh more 266. **GAP Photos** 20; Carole Drake 16; Elke Borkowski 10, 15; FhF Greenmedia 1; Frederic Didillon 252; Friedrich Strauss 24, 161; Gary Smith 25; Jonathan Buckley 253; Lee Avison 11; Robert Mabic 14. **Garden World Images** Dave Bevan 29 above. **Getty Images** Achim Sass 131; Bill Beatty/Visuals Unlimited, Inc. 248; CMB 78; Craig Knowles 185, 187; Dave King 189, 227; David Q. Cavagnaro 73; Deni Brown 94; Dorling Kindersley 174; hazel proudlove 81; Howard Rice 96; John Carey 69; Jonathan Buckley 13; Joshua McCullough 180; Keith Burdett 99; Linda Lewis 278; Mark Bolton 118; Martin Harvey 233; Matthew Ward 153; Maxine Adcock 26; Melina Hammer 211; Neil Fletcher 133; Peter Anderson 19; SilviaJansen 23; Simon Colmer 134; Susie Mccaffrey 21; Valery Rizzo 269; Visuals Unlimited, Inc./Gary Cook 236; Visuals Unlimited, Inc./Scientifica 144; Westend61 107; Yoshio Shinkai 90. **Octopus Publishing Group** David Sarton/Design: del Buono Gazerwitz 7. **Science Photo Library** Geoff Kidd 237. **Shutterstock** ankiro 272; Anna Bogush 164; Basileus 207; Bildagentur Zoonar GmbH 52, 120; Bildagentur Zoonar GmbH 215; Brzostowska 228; canoniroff 196; Colette3 212; D. Kucharski K. Kucharska 44, 111, 124; dabjola 250; Dale Stephens 200; Diana Mower 291; Diana Taliun 218; Dream79 91; Drozdowski 263; eelnosiva 213; Elena Ray 313; Foodpictures 137; Galene 175; giedrius_b 198; Gts 199; hairy mallow 292; Heike Rau 47; Heike Rau 98; hjschneider 113; Hong Vo 106; ID1974 265; I'm Photographer 27; Imageman 76; images72 35; IngridHS 201; Irina Borsuchenko 150; Jessmine 305; joannawnuk 49; Joshua Resnick 181; jreika 264; kanusommer 224, 304; kostrez 123; ksena2you 195; LensTravel 166; LianeM 88, 290; Lilyana Vynogradova 307; Liv friis-larsen 115; macro lens 209; mama_mia 309; marilyn barbone 45, 145, 301; Martien van Gaalen 274; Martin Fowler 42, 216, 311; Mary Terriberry 214; Monika Wisniewska 275; Monkey Business Images 179; Mykyta Voloshyn Voloh 70; Olga Miltsova 157; Paul Cowan 117; Peter Radacsi 40, 56; PHOTO FUN 254; Radka1 72; Robert Biedermann 208; Sarin Kunthong 2, 148; Scisetti Alfio 235; Stocksnapper 204; Sue Robinson 310; SviP 238; Taiftin 297; Taigi 262; Tamara Kulikova 230; Taratorki 273; Tobyphotos 154; Tom Curtis 108; tomtsya 116; troyka 182; ueuaphoto 293; Vahan Abrahamyan 110; Vahan Abrahamyan 172, 176, 247, 306; vaivirga 38, wasanajai 67; Zaneta Baranowska 205; Zdenek Fiamoli 167; zprecech 5. **SuperStock** Biosphoto/ Biosphoto 243; Sudres/Photocuisine 63. **Thinkstock** AlbyDeTweede 89; alfio scisetti 142; alisbalb 27; aodaodaod 193; arnphoto 268; Artush 54; Barbara Dudzi ska 159; BasieB 132; Boarding1Now 55; Brejeq 190; c12 296; Cameron Whitman 188; Carolyn Whamond 50; CGissemann 65; dabjola 36; David Hughes 156; Davidenko Pavel 261; dina2001 282; Du?an Zidar 255; egal 303; Elenathewise 283; feri1 222; fotokon 4, 60; Givaga 83; Grigorii_Pisotckii 68; HandmadePictures 143; Heike Brauer 251; Heike Rau 57; Honorata Kawecka 285; hydrangea100 130; IngridHS 66, 276, 277; inxti 75; Irina Burakova 260; janaph 302; janniwet 48; Jolanta Dabrowska 122; Juanmonino 125; juefraphoto 158; klenova 295; konok1a 267; lnzyx 240; lucagavagna 234; macroart 100; Maksim Shebeko 93; Mari Jensen 178; Mariha-kitchen 97; Mariia Savoskula 162; MIMOHE 59; Nakano Masahiro/amanaimagesRF 136; Nancy Nehring 102; nancykennedy 8; Nicholas Rjabow 82; np-e07 126, 127, 165; Olga Zemlyakova 86; OlgaMiltsova 191, 271; Onur Zongur 210; Pat_Hastings 51; photohomepage 53; photostockam 77; raweenuttapong 104; Robert Biedermann 66; saiko3p 308; SamsonMagnus 34; Santje09 249, 287; sasimoto 42; schmaelterphoto 183; seregam 241; Severas 112; Severga 147; silviacrisman 186; statu-nascendi 62; Stefano Gargiulo 135; stranger28 146; Tamara Kulikova 194; ulkan 219; vau902 284; Vik Borysenko 61; Vitali Dyatchenko 192; VitaSerendipity 80; Vladimir Arndt 140; voltan1 223; YelenaYemchuk 105, 163; Zoonar RF 160; Zoryanchik 229; zyxeos30 239.

Publisher: Alison Starling
Editor: Pollyanna Poulter
Designers: Yasia Williams and Sally Bond
Picture Library Manager: Jennifer Veall
Indexer: Isobel McLean
Production Controller: Allison Gonsalves